You and Your Action Research Project
Second Edition

Jean McNiff, Pamela Lomax and
Jack Whitehead

RoutledgeFalmer
Taylor & Francis Group

LONDON AND NEW YORK

First published 1996, this edn 2003
by RoutledgeFalmer
11 New Fetter Lane, London EC4P 4EE

Simultaneously published in the USA and Canada
by RoutledgeFalmer
29 West 35th Street, New York, NY 10001

RoutledgeFalmer is an imprint of the Taylor & Francis Group

© 2003 Jean McNiff, Pamela Lomax and Jack Whitehead

Typeset in Palatino by BC Typesetting, Bristol
Printed and bound in Great Britain by
MPG Books Ltd.

British Library Cataloguing in Publication Data
A catalogue record for this book is available from the British Library

Library of Congress Cataloging in Publication Data
A catalog record for this book has been requested

ISBN 0–415–31885–8

Contents

PART V
Making claims to knowledge and validating them   129

PART VI
Going public   157

Acknowledgements

We wish to thank Sarah Fletcher, University of Bath, UK, and Máirín Glenn, Inver National School, Ireland, for their painstaking reviews of the book in draft, for their many helpful comments, and for their continuing support.

Introduction

The world we're in

These are exciting times in which to be involved in education, given that major shifts are taking place internationally in what counts as knowledge and who should be seen as a knower. Since the 1970s and 1980s personal practical knowledge has taken its rightful place alongside 'pure' conceptual theory, and practitioners in workplaces have claimed that they are entitled to be regarded as valuable knowledge workers alongside intellectuals in formal settings. Action research has contributed much in getting us to this situation.

The shifts in the knowledge base of education have been accompanied by other, less exciting and deeply troubling shifts. These shifts manifest as a conflict of values about whether human enquiry is to do with having or being (Fromm, 1979). Virtually all human endeavour across the post-industrialised world is caught in the debate, and, given that the post-industrialised world is now characterised as the 'knowledge-creating' world, knowledge itself has been brought into question. People rightly continue to ask important questions about knowledge: Which knowledge is valuable? Whose knowledge is valued? What do we use our knowledge for? Answers depend on values. The conflict is one of whether what we know, who knows, and what we use our knowledge for is about the selfish accumulation and protection of knowledge, power and wealth by minority elites, or whether societies develop and use knowledge for a fairer and more sustainable world for all.

The same issues are now evident in action research, and are highly visible in debates about what counts as action research and who should be regarded as an action researcher. Action research began in the 1940s as a movement in social scientific enquiry that had profound implications for social justice. Over the years refinements took place in the methodological and epistemological base, so that the reasons and intentions of people undertaking their action enquiries were made increasingly clear. Improvements took place in how action research could be validated and justified, and new forms of representation promised even more exciting developments in the field. Throughout the debates, however, the commitment to social justice and a fairer life experience for all remained consistent.

This is now under attack. Action research itself has fallen victim to the technical rational marketisation of knowledge. A new literature has emerged that presents action research as a set of techniques, a 'tool' that aims to ensure specific behavioural 'outcomes'. Books are everywhere with practical advice on how to develop fast-track routes to getting what one wants. Increasingly, what is wanted is improved results, higher achievement scores, and the production of obedient stereotypical consumers. The very idea of action research has changed, from a term that originally communicated the processes of people coming together to work collaboratively to achieve commonly agreed personal and social goals, to a term that now refers to a behavioural process that is as fixed and unchanging as Everest. 'If x, then y' is the formula that underpins traditional social scientific enquiry, a constrained system that, historically, was dislodged by initiatives such as action research. Today, action research itself is dragooned into the service of 'if x, then y' quick-fix solutions.

Thoughtful people know that there are no quick-fix solutions which have lasting benefit for human striving in the interests of fairness for all. It is by patiently and persistently working our way through our dilemmas of social living that we come to situations that, while still far from perfect, hold promise for the possibilities of a better world. These are the commitments out of which we authors write this new edition. The first edition in 1996 was written as contributing to a wider literature that challenged the existing power base of traditional social scientific enquiry. This second edition is written as contributing to a new power base that retains action research as a form of educational enquiry and, drawing on the ideas of Kilpatrick (1951), as a form of dialogue that has profound implications for the future of humanity.

Continuing dilemmas

When we wrote the first edition we explained that we were responding to a need expressed by practitioners for guidance on how to do action research. We had resisted writing a book such as this for a long time. Our resistance was grounded in an anxiety that we might appear to be telling people what to do, while our own commitments are that people can think for themselves and make their own choices, and therefore ask themselves what they should do, and accept the consequences of their actions. Our job, we felt, was to help people ask the kinds of questions that would enable them to be confident in their own capacity for thinking and acting. Our current anxieties are grounded in recent events that have seen a plethora of 'how to do' action research books that not only tell people how to do action research, but also what to do, when to do it, and how to achieve specific results in terms of controlling others' thinking and behaviour.

Our dilemmas therefore continue. We do not wish our work to justify self-contained technical exercises, but we do bear in mind the idea expressed in the first edition that people need to know certain steps before they can dance. We want to continue to encourage people to dance, and to dance in their own way, exploring their own potentials for creativity of spirit and expression, as we do as authors and researchers. We invite you to approach our text in the spirit of an invitation to dance. If you see anything of value in what we are doing, please use it and create your own approach in your own contexts.

We hope you experience our 'telling' how to do action research within an approach that treats as sacred the value of your integrity and creative spirit. We want to relate to you, through our text, in a way that does not violate your integrity. As educators, we are always faced with questions of encouraging people to express values of freedom, democracy, fairness and self-determination, without stifling these qualities through the imposition of inappropriate conceptual structures and power relations. Through our work in higher education, we wish to support the values of truth, honesty, justice and beauty, and to support one another, and other practitioners, in making their contributions to a more peaceful, fair and productive world.

We have written the book in this spirit. Our guiding principle has been the need to share both good practice and the values of the 'good' that motivate people to try to improve their practice. We state throughout that our knowledge is incomplete, in a constant state of restructuring and re-creation. The approaches we share here work for us, as well as for many other people with whom we work. This does not mean that we have got it right. Colleagues the world over offer amended versions of our ideas, and we incorporate those into our work in the same way that they learn from us and adapt our work. This is our experience of being in a dialogical community. That this is the case is shown in this new edition, where we have incorporated new developments in the field into our ideas, without, we hope, jeopardising our own core beliefs about the sanctity of life and the right of all to live and act as they can justify are right for themselves and others.

It is important for us that we communicate this clearly. We are not presenting definitive answers. We are showing how we do action research, in the spirit of modelling our practice, explaining why we act as we do, and inviting you to learn and adapt our work if it is appropriate for you. Throughout we strongly advise that you develop your own strategies, work out your own ideas, perhaps using ours as prompts to get you started. This is not just rhetoric. We can identify changes in ourselves as we have worked together. If you compare previous work of ours, you will see that the ideas in this book are developments and, we argue, improvements from previous times. We claim the right, as action researchers, to change, improve, discard, make errors and enhance our learning. We urge you to do the same.

Audience

Action research is used extensively on pre- and in-service programmes of professional education. It was used initially mainly in teacher education, but today the scope has broadened to include virtually all professions. The range of use has also broadened. It is seen in some contexts as the basis for participatory action for social reform and cultural renewal. It is also seen as a powerful form of organisational and institutional reform. Most literature on professional education draws on the ideas of action research.

We authors are involved in programmes of continuing professional development, mainly in higher education contexts, although we also work in other contexts such as schools and adult education, management and social activism. The examples we offer in the book are drawn from our own experience of supporting action enquiries across the professions, mainly in teacher education. We wish to emphasise however that action research has virtually unlimited scope in relation to the development of personal and professional self-awareness, regardless of context or discipline. Action research, as a form of morally committed action, knows no boundaries other than those that the individual practitioner wishes to construct. We hope that this book is relevant to all contexts of individual and community learning, and we commend it in that spirit.

This second edition of *You and Your Action Research Project* is a practical text that aims to offer concise advice to researchers about how to undertake an action enquiry. It does not contain many examples due to limitations of space, but you can find plenty of examples and case-study material in our other writings and on our websites.

About the authors

Jean McNiff is an independent researcher, living in Dorset and working in international contexts. Much of her work is conducted in Ireland. She is Adjunct Professor at the University of Limerick where she manages and supervises doctoral programmes. She is also a Visiting Fellow at the University of the West of England. Her work has been influential in changing attitudes towards the legitimation of personal professional learning in Ireland and elsewhere. She writes extensively about the power of professional learning for the sustainability of social orders that are animated by a spirit of freedom, fairness, love and beauty for all.

Pamela Lomax was, until July 1997, Professor of Educational Research at Kingston University. She was President of the British Educational Research Association in 1998 and for many years edited their house journal, *Research Intelligence*. She is now an independent educational consultant, supervising research students, lecturing, writing and editing from her home in Cornwall. She has edited a number of books on teacher action research and published many papers on this subject. She is on the editorial board of a number of international journals and is Deputy Editor of *Management in Education*, the house journal of the British Educational, Leadership, Management and Administration Society. Action research remains her main research interest and she brings her expertise in this area to her work supervising Hong Kong students who are registered for doctoral degrees in Educational Leadership and Management at Leicester University.

Jack Whitehead moved to his present position as a lecturer in the Department of Education at the University of Bath in 1973 after six years spent teaching in London comprehensive schools. He is a former President of the British Educational Research Association, Distinguished

Scholar in Residence at Westminster College, Utah, and Visiting Professor at Brock University in Ontario. The main focus of his productive life in education has been to reconstruct what counts as educational theory so that it is focused on the explanations that individuals produce for their learning to live values of humanity more fully in what they are doing. His recent explorations of multi-media representations of embodied values and their transformation into educational standards of judgement may be seen on his award-winning website http://www.actionresearch.net.

You can reach us at:

Jean McNiff: http://www.jeanmcniff.com
Pam Lomax: PamLomax@aol.com
Jack Whitehead: http://www.actionresearch.net

Part I

First principles

Research is about creating new knowledge, finding ways of testing its validity, and sharing the knowledge for specific purposes. In action research terms, those purposes are always to do with learning and personal and social growth.

In Part I we consider the nature of action research, how it is similar to and different from other kinds of research, and what is special about action research that means it leads to personal and social nourishing.

We emphasise throughout that action research is a term which refers to the processes of people conducting their real-life enquiries, as they ask, individually and collectively, 'How do I improve what I am doing for our mutual benefit?'

Chapter 1

The nature of action research

This chapter deals with basic issues about action research. Many of these issues apply to research in general, not only to action research. Action research has specific characteristics that make it different from other kinds of research. The chapter describes the features common to all research, and explains how action research is different; that is, how a research process can be understood as action research and not as something else. It locates action research within the new scholarship, a name given to recent trends in education and social research that place the 'I' at the centre of enquiry processes. This means that action research may be seen as a form of self-study, or first-person enquiry.

The chapter deals with the following questions:

- What is action research, and what is it not?
- How is action research different from other kinds of research?
- How can action research be understood as a new form of scholarship?

What is action research, and what is it not?

We do research when we want to find out something that we did not know before. There are many ways of doing this; action research is one way. Researchers need to be aware that there are different ways of doing research so that they can justify their choice of doing action research. It is important to be clear about the characteristics of all kinds of research to see what is special about action research.

Characteristics of all kinds of research

All research sets out to generate valid evidence to support a claim to new knowledge, that is to say that a person knows something now which was not known before. The new knowledge may take different forms. It can take the objective form of a new discovery or creation, such as the discovery of penicillin or the invention of a new manufacturing process. It can also take a subjective personal form such as when a person comes to understand something that they did not understand previously. Although all kinds of research share the same characteristics, these characteristics tend to be interpreted differently and are often contested. There is always a political dimension to doing research, because researchers have different ideas about what counts as knowledge, and so they also have different ideas about what counts as valid research.

Doing research of any kind involves the following:

Identify a research issue

The issue can be set out in a tightly formulated way, such as a hypothesis to be tested, or in a looser way, such as an idea to be explored.

Identify research aims

The researcher says what he or she hopes to achieve, and why. The research aims are often stated as research questions. The form of these questions varies according to the kind of research chosen. Questions of the kind, 'What is happening here?', which are asked in traditional qualitative research, are different from questions of the kind, 'How do I improve my work?' (Whitehead, 1989), which are the kinds of questions asked in action research. In traditional qualitative research, the researcher stands outside the research and observes what other people are doing. In action research, the researcher is the centre of the research, and the focus is on self-improvement.

Set out a research design

The research design may be understood as the overall plan. It explains how the research will be conducted. Will it be conducted according to a fixed set of action steps, or in a developmental way, where new ideas may be explored as they emerge?

Gather data

All research involves observation and keeping records of what is happening. This data gathering refers to what is happening in the research process. Firsthand data are 'raw' data about the immediate situation, such as photographs or tape-recorded conversations. Secondhand data are derivative and are contained in reports or other documents about the research.

Set success criteria

Criteria need to be identified to show how the data may be judged in relation to the research aims. In traditional types of research, these criteria tend to be fixed from the start, and relate to specified aims and objectives. In newer types of research, such as action research, they may emerge as the research proceeds and relate to the values that inform the research.

Generate evidence from the data

This involves interpreting the data to show how they relate to the criteria. If they do, the data take on a new status as evidence. Always remember that evidence is not the same as data (see page 63).

Make a claim to knowledge

Based on the evidence, making a claim to knowledge means showing how new knowledge has been generated, and why the knowledge should now count as legitimate knowledge. The claim is not necessarily related to whether or not the research influenced external circumstances, or had other implications. The claim relates to the new knowledge and its potential validity.

Link new knowledge with existing knowledge

Once it has been created, the new knowledge is placed within the existing body of knowledge, so that the claim may be perceived as a new contribution, not a repetition of what has gone before. It therefore adds to the existing body of knowledge, usually in the form of a report that can be referenced by other researchers.

Submit the claim to critique

So that the claim is not regarded simply as an opinion, it is necessary to obtain feedback from others about the validity of the claim.

Disseminate the findings

This involves making the research process and its findings available to wider audiences so that it can now count as public knowledge.

The above are features common to all kinds of research.

How is action research different from other kinds of research?

Action research is different from other kinds of research in the following ways.

It is practitioner based

Action research is conducted by practitioners who regard themselves as researchers. It is therefore also called practitioner research, practitioner-led research and practitioner-based research. It is also called action enquiry. (Action learning is different, although the distinctions between action research and action learning have become increasingly blurred. Action research involves making public an explanatory account of practice.) In health and social care contexts, terms such as 'user-research' or 'service-user-led research' are used (see Winter and Munn-Giddings, 2001). The practitioner base to action research means that all people in all contexts who are investigating the situation they are in can become researchers, regardless of their age, status, social setting, or social or professional positioning. The situations may be in virtually any context – in the workplace, in the home, in an aeroplane – and in any personal or professional arena. Because action research is always done by practitioners within a particular social situation, it is insider research (not outsider research), which means that the researcher is inside the situation, and will inevitably influence what is happening.

In some forms of interpretive action research, however, people believe it is appropriate for an external researcher to stand outside the situation and watch others doing their action research. The external researcher then writes about the situation, checking his or her interpretations with participants. While this book includes an interpretive perspective, it is written out of a value that participants should evaluate their own practices rather than try to evaluate someone else's.

It focuses on learning

Action research is about individuals' learning, in company with other people. People are always in relation with others in some way. Relationships are important, because an improvement in personal practice usually involves a deeper understanding of oneself in relation with others.

Action research is different from social scientific research which aims to understand and describe an external situation. Action research is a process that helps you, a practitioner, to develop a deeper understanding about what you are doing as an insider researcher. Action research has both a personal and a social aim. The personal aim is the improvement of your own learning, while the social aim is an improvement of your situation. Both are equally important and interdependent. Your report is an account of how your learning developed through studying your practice within the situation, and how your learning influenced the situation. It does not matter if the social situation does not reach successful closure; it probably will not because any solution allows new questions to emerge. What does matter is that you show your own process of learning, and explain how your new learning has helped you to develop your work within the situation. (Unfortunately, some agencies that support action research these days expect concrete 'outcomes' in terms of externally imposed targets, a trend that potentially constrains learning and distorts the research process – see Introduction.)

It embodies good professional practice, and goes beyond

When people do action research for the first time they often say, 'This is what I do in any case.' To an extent, this is so. We act, reflect on our actions, and modify our practice in the light of what we learn. This is good professional practice, which emphasises the action (often problem solving), but it is not action research. Action research is more than problem solving, and involves identifying the reasons for the action which are related to the researcher's values, and gathering and interpreting data to show that the reasons and values were justified and fulfilled. Good professional practice emphasises the action but does not always question the motives. To be action research, there must be praxis which embodies practice. Praxis is informed, committed action that gives rise to knowledge as well as successful action. It is informed because other people's views and feelings are taken into account. It is committed and intentional in terms of values that have been examined and may be argued.

It can lead to personal and social improvement

We said in the Introduction that we believe people (severe pathology aside) are capable of learning (to be more precise, they are incapable of not learning), and should accept the responsibility of thinking and acting for themselves, starting by focusing on their own practice within their situation. This means that people commit to evaluating their own work and finding ways of improving it with a view to influencing others. Self-evaluation enables people to hold themselves accountable for what they think and do. The idea of social change is embodied in the processes of groups of individuals who are committed to changing the way they think and act. Individual practitioners can become dynamic change agents who can generate wide-scale social change by working together. Action research is a form of personal enquiry, but it is always done collaboratively because it involves individuals working together to achieve commonly agreed goals.

It is responsive to social situations

People do action research when they want to investigate what is happening in their particular situation and try to improve it. They not only observe and describe what is happening; they also take action. They begin by trying to understand how they are positioned within their particular situation, and whether what they are doing is in accord with their values. They try to understand how they might improve what they are doing, on the assumption that their decision to improve the situation, beginning with themselves, will enable them to influence others in their contexts, in accordance with their values. They do not aim to change other people. They aim to change themselves by questioning what they are doing, evaluating it rigorously, and explaining to others how their personal improvement can contribute to social improvement.

It demands high order questioning

They begin this process by questioning the assumptions that underlie their practice and their situation. Action research may not be problem solving (bringing an investigation to closure), but it does imply problem posing (or problematising); that is, not accepting things at face value. This involves questioning at several levels. These levels are often called 'first, second and third order learning'. First order learning refers to learning about a situation: for example, 'How many women managers are in the firm?' Second order learning is learning to question what has been learned: 'How can we involve more women managers?' Third order learning is learning to ask why the situation is as it is, and why one might need to change the way one thinks about it: 'Why is it necessary to ask questions about the involvement of women managers in the first place?' Developing this type of critical perspective means recognising that situations are not 'given', but are created by people with particular intentions over time. The research project might unearth issues which seemingly have nothing to do with its original aims, yet are important to under-standing the situation with a view to changing it.

It is intentionally political

Deciding to take action is itself a political act, because what one person does invariably has consequences for someone else. Action researchers need to understand that they are frequently in potentially politically con-tested scenarios. When practitioners begin to question the current and historical contexts of a situation, and perhaps begin to reveal injustices, they have to make decisions about whether they wish to follow their own value commitments and try to improve the situation according to what they believe in, or whether they will go along with the status quo. These are difficult decisions to make and can involve personal discomfort. The affirmation that one has contributed to social development, however, can be a powerful incentive to act in the interests of social justice.

The focus is on change, and the self is the locus of change

Situations do not change themselves. People change, and they change their situations. Change begins in people's minds, so that when people decide to do something about their work, they set up a process of personal change (individual learning) that can transform into a process of social change (collective learning). Traditional kinds of research usually stop at the level of describing a situation. They sometimes go on to suggest ways in which the situation might be changed. Action researchers take action, and begin by asking, 'What can I do? How do I do it?'

Practitioners accept responsibility for their own actions

In traditional types of research, researchers usually carry out what is required by someone else, such as policy makers or funders. They may make decisions about research procedures, but they do not make decisions about the aims of the research. Action researchers make their own decisions about what is important and what they should do. This is a massive responsibility, because researchers then base their decisions for action on how they understand what is good, and how they think the world should be. They use their values as the basis for their action. Because this is such a massive responsibility they always need to check whether theirs are justifiable values, whether they are living in the direc-tion of their values, and whether their influence is benefiting other people in ways that those other people also feel are good. This involves highly rigorous evaluation checks and restraints, to make sure that action researchers can justify, and do not abuse, their potential influence.

It emphasises the values base of practice

Action research begins with practitioners becoming aware of what is important to them – their values – and how they might act in the direction of those values. Action research is value laden, which differs from the neutral stance claimed for some other types of research. Action research becomes a process of living in a way that practitioners feel is right. This has serious implications for issues of justification and validation of research findings (see Chapters 9 and 10).

How can action research be understood as a new form of scholarship?

Since the 1940s, considerable shifts have been taking place in the knowledge base of social and education research. The term 'knowledge base' refers to ideas about what counts as knowledge, how the knowledge is tested to ensure its validity, and what it looks like in terms of its products. This has considerable implications for who counts as a knower, and why.

From about the 1940s, and for a long time before that, though less noticeably so, movements had been afoot to dislodge the stranglehold of traditional approaches that emphasised technical rational forms of knowing. These movements appeared as new forms of research that were qualitative rather than only quantitative; new areas of investigation appeared that were concerned with human experience rather than only behavioural performance; and practitioners as well as intellectuals came to be regarded as researchers. These new, more inclusive forms of research concentrated on understanding the relationships among people, and between people and their environments. They used methodologies that offered descriptions and explanations of the experience of practice, instead of aiming to predict and control potential outcomes. Research was no longer a search for one objective Truth, but the creation of multiple truths that communicated varieties of pluralistic and democratic living. Practitioners were now acknowledged as legitimate knowledge workers. Democracy in research was coming of age.

These different traditions have been variously described as 'old' and 'new' paradigm research, and the 'old' and 'new' scholarship. There is little difference between what the terms communicate, and they are used interchangeably in this book. What continues to be interesting are the attitudes of researchers working in the different traditions. While most people get along amicably, serious hostilities can break out when people feel their territory is threatened, understandably enough, because for many people territory symbolises intellectual and physical property, and therefore status and income.

Action research is part of the new scholarship. It emphasises the idea of knowledge generation as creative practice that evolves through dialogue. It recognises knowledge not only as an outcome of cognitive activity, but also as embodied; that is, mind and body are not perceived as separate entities but as integrated. Knowledge is arrived at, and exists in, feelings and multiple sensory modes. Consequently knowledge exists as much 'in here' as 'out there'.

The new scholarship covers many different disciplines and areas of enquiry, but its significance and implications are far-reaching. Human enquiry and now moved to finding better ways of living together to sustain ourselves and the planet, and recognises that social and environmental well-being can happen only when individual people make deliberate commitments to working together to achieve their democratically negotiated goals.

We continue these themes in Chapter 2, and offer a summary of the main features of action research.

Chapter 2

The main features of action research processes

This chapter summarises the main features of action research processes. The ideas are developed throughout the book, and can provide important theoretical frameworks for your practical work.

Summary of the main features of action research

Action research involves	These ideas are developed in
1 A commitment to educational improvement 2 A special kind of research question 3 Putting the 'I' at the centre of the research 4 Action that is informed, committed and intentional	} Part II
	Part III shows how the ideas come together in the processes of action planning
5 Systematic monitoring to generate valid data 6 Authentic descriptions of the action 7 Explaining the action	} Part IV
8 New ways of representing research 9 Validating action research claims	} Part V
10 Making the action research public	Part VI

1 A commitment to educational improvement

Education does not mean teaching or instruction, though it can involve these practices. In our view, education refers to the interaction between people (and other beings) which enables them to grow in life-affirming ways. The 'aim' of education is to enable mental, physical and spiritual growth (Dewey, 1938). Education may therefore be understood as embodied in the relationships between people. When these relationships help people to live in life-affirming ways they may be termed *educative relationships*. People who help other people to grow are educators. This means that people in all professions and settings, regardless of status, can be educators. Educative relationships provide the types of context in which people feel enabled to learn. Action researchers aim to develop educative relationships to enable all participants to learn and grow. This is why the focus is on the individual practitioner, as they ask questions of the kind, 'How do I improve what I am doing?' (Whitehead, 1989); 'How do I help you to learn?' (Russell and Korthagen, 1995); and 'How do I improve what I am doing for our mutual benefit?' (see page 7).

Action research is an intervention in personal practice to encourage improvement for oneself and others. The action is not haphazard or routine, but driven by educational values that need to be explored and defended. It is a practical form of research which recognises that the world is not perfect and that professional values have to be negotiated. It also recognises that, while the focus may be the individual practitioner, individuals are always in company with others. So a central value that is accepted by most action researchers is the value of respect for other people, which means that those people's views and values must be accommodated.

2 A special kind of research question

The special kind of research question that action researchers ask begins:

> How do I . . .

and continues with questions that have educational intent:

> . . . understand my practice better (for your benefit)?
> . . . help you to learn?
> . . . contribute to the wider body of knowledge?
> . . . contribute to the education of social formations?

In action research there is a clear intent to intervene in and improve one's own understanding and practice, and to accept responsibility for oneself.

The aim is not to assume responsibility for improving others. The aim is to improve yourself, appreciating that you are always in relation with others, so the quality of your influence may be assessed in terms of how others respond to your practice. You ask, 'How do I . . .?' because action research should be about your action, not the action of others (see page 30 for examples).

(*must be I*)

3 Putting the 'I' at the centre of the research

You are the person at the centre of the research. Action research reports use 'I' as the author, and reports often take the form of personal stories. Action research is first-person research ('I/we did . . .'). Third-person accounts, which are appropriate for traditional research reports ('the researcher did . . .'), are to be avoided. New traditions are emerging in action research that encourage people to use fictional writing and other forms of representation to explain their work (see page 169).

The emphasis on the living person 'I' shows how individuals can take responsibility for improving and sustaining themselves, and the world they are in. 'I' have the capacity to influence the process of social change in this way, because 'I' can influence others in my immediate context, who in turn can influence others in their contexts. The circles of influence are potentially without limit. Collectively, individuals can generate world-wide change.

How do 'I' fit into the research?

- I am the subject and object of the research.
- I take responsibility for my own actions.
- I own my claims and judgements.
- I am the author of my own research accounts.

How do 'I' fit into the action?

- I see my practice as the central focus of my research through critical reflection and study.
- I encourage others to participate in a negotiated living definition of shared practices.
- I show respect for other opinions and other ways of doing things.
- I show humility and expose my vulnerability.
- I am open to argument.
- I am willing to accept that I might be wrong and might need to change my ideas.
- I own my mistakes.
- I stand my ground when my principles are at stake.

How do 'I' influence wider social contexts?

- I accept responsibility for investigating how I can improve my own work for others' benefit.
- I encourage others to do the same.
- We engage in collaborative practices to create cultures of enquiry.
- We share our knowledge and disseminate our ideas.
- We create ourselves as groups of critically reflective practitioners and scholars who are committed to securing freedom and fairness for all.
- Our aim is to contribute to the development of social formations through education.

4 Action that is informed, committed and intentional

Action research involves *informed*, *committed* and *intentional* action. These elements turn practice into praxis.

Informed action

The 'action' of action research is always informed; that is, it does not 'just happen'. The process might begin with a hunch, or a felt need to do something about a particular issue. Deciding to do something about it means actively questioning your own motives and actions, treating your findings and interpretations critically, suspending your judgements, and being open to other people's points of view. You do need to accept that other people might be better informed. Winter and Munn-Giddings (2001: 212) talk about 'reflective critique'. They say that when other people 'do not understand' us, an immediate reaction is to reply that their lack of understanding is their problem. However, if we want to learn, we need to ask, 'What is it that I do not understand about them that leads me to perceive them as "not understanding" something?' We need to question the view that we have all the answers. While we might passionately commit to our own values, we always need to recognise that we might be mistaken (Polanyi, 1958) and still have much to learn from others. Finding the balance between conviction and open-mindedness can be difficult, and involves personal honesty.

Committed action

Having made a decision to act, you then need to get on with it. Your action stems from a strong personal conviction that things could be better. You are not acting out of a selfish desire to have things your own way, or to manipulate others, or out of a mandate to implement others' ideas. You are committed to your own values and how you might live in the direction of those values. This means that you constantly evaluate what you are doing, and check, through rigorous validation procedures (Chapter 9), that you are acting honestly and openly for the benefit of others, so that the project does not become an exercise in self-delusion.

Intentional action

Action research is intentional. The experience of doing a project can also be chaotic (Griffiths, 1990; Mellor, 1998; Ó Muimhneacháin, 2002). Some people take the view that action research aims to bring an unsatisfactory situation to closure (see page 145). Others, including the authors, take the view that the process of doing action research, and the learning generated, is as important (possibly more important) than any final solution (which will probably generate more questions anyway) (see also Atkinson, 2000). In our opinion, asking questions with a view to improvement can reveal the hidden complexities of a situation and allow important dilemmas to be surfaced and addressed, and help us to learn how to find a way through, or to live with them.

5 Systematic monitoring to generate valid data

An important outcome of your action research will be your changed understanding of your practice, and your understanding of how this has happened. Being systematic about collecting data is important for many aspects of the research process. Being systematic involves collecting data so that you can pinpoint where your evaluation of your action has led to new insights about your practice. Being systematic about monitoring and evaluating your action will help you make explicit the points at which learning takes place. Collecting data can involve tricky decisions because it is not always possible to predict which data will be important later on. Being systematic means that data collecting is not random, but should be done according to some plan. It should be as comprehensive as possible because many important insights develop after the event, as you try to make sense of the data you have collected. The data can be turned into evidence to show these changes in understanding. Part IV gives advice about the sorts of data you might collect and how you can deal with it.[1]

1 The word 'data' is commonly used in both singular and plural forms: 'data is' and 'data are'. Technically the plural form is correct. Both forms are used in this book as seems appropriate to the context.

6 Authentic descriptions of the action

It is important to be clear about the differences between description and explanation. Descriptions give accounts of activities that have happened, and usually take the form of reports. They are written in hindsight; that is, they give a report of what has happened, even if the time lag is minimal. Explanations are the processes of making sense of what has happened, when you reflect on the reported action and give reasons for why it is happening. The reasons are often given in terms of values. Think about what sports commentators do. First they describe what is happening (the actions) and then they offer their analyses of the actions (their explanations). It is important not to jeopardise the authenticity of your work and lose focus by confusing descriptions of the data with your explanations.

This section deals with descriptions. Section 7 deals with explanations.

Descriptions take many forms. Some of the most common are as follows:

Factual accounts

Most descriptions of action are factual accounts. They are often based on transcripts of conversations and meetings, or summaries of data from questionnaires and interviews. Often statistical summaries are included to show the number and quality of events and phenomena, such as inter-actions between people at meetings, or individual opinions, or preferences and trends. Contrary to some opinions, statistical data can be important elements in action research accounts (see pages 118–121 for examples).

Multimedia approaches

Video and audio tape-recordings are important ways of gathering factual data. Exciting developments in the use of multimedia technologies are setting new precedents. Often it is impossible to capture the full impact of events through purely verbal reports. The meaning of the action can often be communicated better using visual or other sensory modes. For example, the idea that 'Mary was enthusiastic' might be communicated more effectively by showing a clip from a video rather than the bare presentation of words. The website http://www.actionresearch.net is a powerful resource to show these ideas in practice, and will also put you in touch with other websites around the world.

Subjective accounts

Other descriptions may be based on more subjective accounts taken from diaries and personal reflections and observations. These are subjective only in the sense that they represent one person's viewpoint. It could be that they have been produced more systematically and with less bias than the more 'objective' accounts described above.

Fictionalised accounts

Many action researchers use fictionalised accounts that can preserve the anonymity of participants. Anonymity is important, for example, in projects that look at staff development or appraisal when the real identities of people should be protected. Some researchers have written stories that enable them to open up to public discussion events that would be too confidential to report; for example, some aspects of managers' meetings. These fictionalised accounts may be written so that the context is changed or the characters are given identities that mask their real identity (see Dadds and Hart, 2001, for some excellent accounts that adopt this approach). Presenting your work as fiction can often give it an impact that is not communicated in more factual accounts (see p. 169). Stories are increasingly recognised as communicating the processes of research. Read the work of Jean Clandinin and Michael Connelly (2000) on narrative inquiry for further ideas.

7 Explaining the action

You need to explain the action (give your analyses) once you have described it. This will involve you in:

- identifying possible meanings, linking with other work, and constructing models;
- making the description problematic;
- theorising.

Identifying possible meanings, linking with other work and constructing models

While action research can (but need not) include testing hypotheses and applying other people's theories and models to your work, you should aim to read the literature and incorporate relevant insights into your theorising. If you are on an award-bearing course, you will be expected to engage critically with the literature. You should explain why you agree or disagree with other people's theories and do or do not use them in your work, and you should explain why you are developing theories and models of your own and why these are appropriate for you.

Making the description problematic

Taking a critical stance towards your action and its outcomes is an essential piece of coming to an explanation. This is important in action research where 'being subjective' can be both an advantage and a limitation. It can be an advantage because you have an insider knowledge of events. It can be a limitation because you may come to biased conclusions about what you are doing. Therefore you need to be systematic in questioning both your motives for action and your evaluation of its outcomes. To get a reasonably unprejudiced view you need to involve other people who will act as critical friends to critique your interpretations. It is important to try to get good data that can be discussed and analysed.

Theorising

Offering explanations is the ground for creating your own theory of what you are doing. Your theory of practice is your explanation of why you are doing things the way you are. You are making your practice problematic by questioning taken-for-granted assumptions (your own and others'), and by questioning the extent to which you are living your values in your practice. You are stating your reasons for action in terms of your values, and showing how you can justify your action in terms of what you believe is a right way of living. You can then go on to show the potential significance of your theory for wider social and political debates. Your theory is created from within your work and represents your present best thinking. It is always developing, because you are always in the process of development. Your theory is not static; it is living, part of your life. It is your own living theory (Whitehead, 1989, 1993). If your theory shows how your work can be understood as educational, you can claim that you are creating your own living educational theory (see page 164 for further discussion).

8 New ways of representing research

Traditional forms of theory are usually presented as analyses of what is known (existing knowledge), and are usually offered in writing. They then appear as statements about concepts. These statements constitute conceptual forms of theory. People's personal practical theories are presented as work in progress (developing knowledge), and appear as statements about human experience. They constitute living forms of theory. While these theories are also usually written, they may also be presented using forms other than writing (see page 168 for new developments in the field).

New ways of presenting written accounts

Written accounts use different techniques to show the living processes of coming to understand, and the generation of theory. These include:

- self-reflective writing, often in the form of diaries and logs;
- written conversations;
- narrative and story.

Self-reflective writing

This usually appears as diaries and logs. Diaries may be kept as records of events and also of reflections on those events and consequent learning. It might be useful to organise the page (perhaps divide it in two) to record what happened, and then record what you learned. On the left side write 'What happened' and on the right side write 'What I learned'.

Self-reflection may be understood as a conversation with oneself. Barrie Jones (1989) uses an interesting technique in which he engages himself in a conversation to show the process of how his understanding of his action research developed. He writes:

> Introduced by Diamond (1988) to the idea of using biography as a tool for self-understanding, my interest in this approach was given momentum by a book written by Boud and Griffin (1987) in which they discuss the potential of standing away from the process of one's learning in order to tease out and crystallise the development therein. These inputs stimulated my thinking and led me eventually to the idea of concocting an 'imaginary' friend, an interlocutor who would become a springboard for my self-reflection.
>
> (Jones, 1989: 47)

Using conversation and dialogue

We all have conversations all the time. Conversations take place in face-to-face encounters, and they also take place with people who are invisible or distant in space and time. We have conversations with people who write books and articles, who create the buildings we live in, who appear on TV. These conversations are one-sided, not dialogical; we respond to people, but we get no response in return. Dialogical conversations are those in which all parties attempt to respond to others in ways that will enable the conversation to continue. This form of dialogue can help in creating one's own theory of practice. In presenting our theories of practice, it is essential also to show the processes involved. Work is now available to show these processes; for example, Larter's (1987) and Shobbrook's (1997) dissertations are presented entirely in dialogical form. Kevin McDermott (2002) wrote his doctoral thesis on the creation of conversational classrooms.

Using narrative and story

Stories are another way of representing action research. These stories tend to resist closure. They tell the processes of coming-to-know, and share people's thinking, and they are generative, because they show the potential for further development. Stories may be presented both as formative progress reports (work in progress, theories in development) and also as summative reports, dissertations and theses (reports of current thinking, theories in action). When you present your progress report, whether orally or in writing, you must have your data available to show how your personal development is always in relation to what other participants in the research are thinking and doing. Your final report will probably appear in written form, but should include the 'live' evidence of your interactions and conversations with other people, to show how you exercised your educative influence in their lives. This live evidence may appear in non-written form, such as in CD-ROMs and interactive texts, and these would be included as part of the written text and as appendices or archived materials.

New ways of representing non-written accounts

Non-written forms are becoming increasingly accepted. They include the following:

Visual models and diagrams

These appear everywhere in the literature. They aim to communicate the reality of particular structures and processes, and show their underlying ideas. It is important to see these models for what they are; that is, models created by people to communicate their vision of reality. Bourdieu (1990) cautions against confusing the model with the reality it is supposed to represent. The model is not the reality; it aims to represent reality. When you see diagrams, always question whether they offer explanations for your life, or whether you could create your own explanations to communicate the reality of your life more appropriately.

Models also communicate the values that inform their creators' thinking. In our view, the models that communicate most effectively the creative nature of action research are those that try to represent the fluidity of open-ended, free enquiry. We try to communicate our ideas using the verbal models that form the basis for the enquiry processes outlined in this book (see pages 59) , and diagrams such as Figure 2.1 (See McNiff with Whitehead, 2000, 2002).

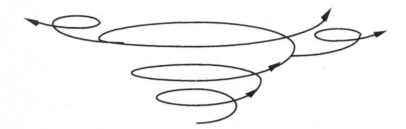

Figure 2.1 A generative transformational evolutionary process

Drawings

These can be a powerful way of creating unique visualisations that can help you to understand and communicate changes in your action research. A number of these are explained in Lomax and Parker (1995). Exciting new ideas are developing such as the use of snake charts as part of semi-structured interviews (Parker, 1994). Mary Roche (2000) encouraged her children to use drawings to chart their own processes of thinking.

Using experiential techniques

Researchers are using different forms of experience to support people in exploring different ways of knowing. Practitioners are invited to engage in varieties of experience, based on the idea of multiple intelligences, to explore their different ways of knowing. Have a look at the Image and Identity Research Collective of Sandra Weber and Claudia Mitchell at http://www.iire.mcgill.ca. See also the work of Máirín Glenn at http://www.iol.ie/~bmullets.

9 Validating action research claims

Validation involves:

- making claims;
- examining critically the claims against evidence;
- involving others in the validation process.

In old scholarship research, it is assumed that validity can be established for those things that can be known objectively (see e.g. Popper, 1963, 1972). A traditional form of logic (way of thinking) is used to test the consistency of arguments. This kind of formal logic is inadequate for action research, because action research emphasises the importance of the person's own interpretations and negotiation of events. The kinds of logic used in action research are both dialectical and propositional as the explanations make sense of shifting experiences while drawing on insights from traditional scholarship. Validity is established by showing how interpretations of experience can be negotiated by different people. This can happen on a number of levels:

- *Self-validation:* The initial validation of action research depends on the kind of explanation of their practices that individuals are willing to offer themselves.
- *Peer validation:* A second level occurs when co-practitioners, persons who understand the context in which we operate, can work vicariously through the evidence we provide to understand the claims we make.
- *Wider public validation:* A third level is going public, convincing others who may be strangers about the truth of our claims.

Validation is a system that should be part of the ongoing, formative processes of action research. This is part of critical, self-reflective processes. It operates when action researchers discuss their work informally with colleagues, critical friends and tutors. It can also be a more formal event and part of a summative evaluation process (see page 133). It can also be very formal, as in the presentation of a paper to an audience at a conference or the publication of an account of the research in a refereed journal.

Making claims

Making a claim to knowledge means saying that something is known now that was not known before. What types of claim do action researchers make? They make claims about what they have come to know through studying their practice. It is important (and often overlooked) to make claims about the research (what you have come to know), and not only about the action (what you have done). Presumably the action would have happened irrespective of the research focus. Placing the action within a research framework has added something that makes the claim different from what it would have been had the claim been regarded simply as the outcome of good professional practice.

What the research framework has added may be understood in terms of the kind of questions that action researchers ask.

How do I improve . . .

. . . my personal practice?
. . . my understanding of this?
. . . the wider educational situation?

The answers to these questions may be framed as claims, for example:

Through the research I

. . . understand what I did not know before.
. . . have changed my practice so that it is more educational.
. . . have encouraged people to do things differently in ways that can be shown to be better than before.

Validation processes enable action researchers to test their claims that they have improved their practice and understand better what they are doing, and why they are doing it, such as motivating frequently absent students or colleagues to turn up to work, or enabling people to become more reflective about their work.

Some action researchers will also be able to demonstrate how they have influenced organisational change in a way that represents real educational improvement, such as implementing a new policy successfully or arranging for more participation in decision making (see e.g. Bosher, 2001; Delong, 2002).

Critically examining the claims against evidence

Doing action research involves regular validation procedures such as recording personal reflections in a journal, and meetings where people gather to consider the claims that the researcher is making. Meetings should never take the form of cosy chats, where everyone aims to reach agreement, though they should always be supportive. Validation meetings aim to encourage researchers to think about their work critically, and to find ways of improving it where necessary. Validation meetings enable researchers to:

- test out arguments with a critical audience who will challenge lack of clarity, help identify weaknesses and suggest modifications;
- consider data and the way it is analysed and presented;
- sharpen claims to knowledge and make sure the data support them;
- develop new ideas;

- generate enthusiasm to continue the research;
- draw on others' support and solidarity.

Always regard validation meetings as working meetings that you can learn from. Do not be defensive, but use the experience to move your work forward.

Some common pitfalls

Researchers often commit the following errors:

- They fail to separate description and explanation: they describe the action rather than say why they did what they did and what they learned from the process.
- They confuse data and evidence: they present the raw data without summarising it or showing its relationship to the criteria they use in their claim to know (see page 143).
- They do not record the meeting: a validation meeting that tests claims to knowledge is an integral part of the research process.

Involving others in the validation process

Most researchers aim to keep track of their research by setting up validation groups. These are groups of people who come together to listen to the researcher describe what he or she is doing and offer possible explanations to show how and why the research is going to enable him or her to make an original claim to knowledge. The group looks at the data gathered so far, and considers the way that the researcher is going to turn the data into evidence (see page 64). They can make suggestions about how the research might proceed. The composition of these validation groups is important. Ideally they should contain people who variously:

- know the context of the work or are able to empathise with the context;
- come from outside the context and can provide an outsider view, to complement those who are within the context;
- are familiar with the methodology of action research but not necessarily with the situation in which it is undertaken.

This discussion continues in Part V.

10 Making the action research public

Making public does not only mean publishing in a journal or giving a paper at a conference, though these are traditional academic ways.

Making public means sharing ideas and findings with other people, particularly colleagues in the work context, and checking with them whether your findings are reasonably fair and accurate. You should not leave going public until the end of the project. Aim to go public throughout the process of the research to keep checking the validity of your accounts and to help your enquiry move forward.

Making research public is the best way of getting it validated. It indicates that you have nothing to hide and are willing for others to scrutinise what has happened in order to help you develop your thinking. You can learn a great deal from listening to questions from people who are outside the research. These questions may help you to strengthen your convictions about the claims you have made and find better evidence to convince others about them, or, as is more often the case, they may lead you to modify your claims because you are able to identify gaps in your arguments that you had not seen before. 'Going public' can be an exciting aspect of action research, because other people would share similar concerns as yourself and express their support and enthusiasm. Support can be very important in research processes.

Making public also has its difficulties. You need to consider important ethical issues if you intend to publish information that involves others. It is particularly important to ensure confidentiality and anonymity in action research. It is also particularly difficult because action research by definition is about yourself and therefore others can identify themselves and one another through you. Being completely open about the research from the beginning can pre-empt many of the problems that can arise when people are secretive about what they are doing. In the past some researchers have found themselves unable to report some of their work because it involves colleagues who had no idea they were included and rightly refused permission for the research to go ahead when they found out.

Making public is part of the discipline of action research because it invites corroboration and critique. You will have to consider how you want people to judge your research. Do you want them to judge it in terms of its relevance and usefulness to their own practice? Do you want them to be convinced that you have found a way of improving your own practice? Do you want them to check whether you have behaved professionally and ethically? Do you want them to appreciate how you have exercised your educative influence? Whatever criteria you choose to focus on, you will need to provide good evidence to support what you are saying, and the quality of your evidence will depend on the quality of your data. Making public means situating your research in its social context; that is, showing that the research is part of the real world, and then sharing the findings of your research with other people.

Conclusion

These ideas are potted summaries of the main characteristics of action research. They can act as reference points as you work your way through this book and through your project. Part III explains how the ideas inform the processes of action planning.

Now you need to think in practical terms of getting on with your action research project. Before you begin the project, however, you need to consider how you are going to work with others and how you are going to develop a plan for conducting your project. These issues are dealt with in Part II.

Part II

Before you begin . . .

Before you begin, think about how you are going to tackle the whole project. You need to assess realistically where you are, what you hope to achieve, and how you think you might get there. This is a vital reconnaissance phase because action research is about people researching their own practice in company with other people within real-world situations, so you need to consider the degree to which you will involve other people in your project and how smooth you believe your path will be.

Working with people is complex, and involves a high level of interpersonal awareness. It also usually means working in institutional settings, and this involves a certain level of political awareness. You and your colleagues probably work within established organisational structures, and these structures might present obstacles and constraints to your plans. You need to be aware of the potential difficulties in advance so that you can build up the necessary resources to cope if the occasion arises.

You should also bear in mind that you are constantly influencing people. You need to be clear about how you intend to exercise your influence, and what kind of influence you hope to exercise. This means you have to be constantly alert to ethical considerations and to make your own decisions about the degree to which you believe you should implement them.

Once you have done this important thinking work, you can begin to plan your project.

Chapter 3

Working with others in organisational and institutional settings

This chapter is in three parts:

- Working with people at an interpersonal level: basic principles of working successfully with others
- Working with people in organisational and institutional settings: advice about what you should do to ensure that your project has a reasonably good chance of success
- Possible implications: what you might decide about conducting your project

Before you begin, be aware that certain basic principles relate to working with people at an interpersonal level and also to working with people in formal settings. They are:

1 *Be optimistic and be realistic.* You are probably doing your research because you believe it is possible to do something useful. Your sense of what is possible can be obstructed however by the realities of what is not possible. You may feel it is possible to influence a situation, but you may find that constraints prevent you from doing this. The constraints can be in the form of people and their interests, and also in the established structures and processes of organisational life. Have faith that you can overcome the constraints and realise the possible from within the seemingly impossible.

2 *Be sensitive to the situation and be strategic.* You need to develop a good sense of what people are feeling, and how well your work is being accepted within the organisation. Unless you are sensitive to your contexts, you are probably not going to get very far. Develop strategies

that will help you deal with whatever situation arises. This means consciously building up a repertoire of coping strategies, and using them.
3   *Be flexible and stay focused.* Aim to adapt to circumstances as they arise,
both in terms of people's needs and wishes, and also in terms of situational changes. If you cannot adapt to changing circumstances, you
will probably go under. At the same time, stay focused on what you
want, and find new directions if your initial plans are not successful.

Working with people at an interpersonal level

This section identifies the main groups of people with whom you are likely
to work, and the kinds of attitude and behaviour you should develop to
keep them on your side.

Groups of people

The main groups of people with whom you are likely to work are as
follows.

Research participants

These are often the people with whom you work. Your research cannot
happen without your participants, so never abuse their goodwill. You are
researching your practice, and finding ways of improving yourself for the
benefit of yourself and your participants. You are the main source of
data for your project, because you are investigating your own work. You
will ground your claims to personal improvement in terms of how you
have influenced others in an educative way, so they also become sources
of data. Pay close attention to all matters of access and confidentiality.
Keep your participants informed about how your research is going.
Invite their feedback, and let them know it is valued. Thank them
frequently; affirmation goes further than any other incentive. You cannot
afford not to let your participants know they are valued.

Your critical friend(s) (or another term such as 'critical colleague')

These are often drawn from the people with whom you are working.
They may also be external to your situation. Your critical friends should
be willing to discuss your work sympathetically but critically. You and
your critical friends choose each other, so you need to negotiate the
ground rules of your relationship. They may turn out to be your closest
allies, so never take them for granted. As well as expecting support
from your friends, you must also be prepared to support them in return.
This means being available, even in antisocial hours, offering as well as

receiving advice, even if it is painful or unwelcome, and always aiming to praise and support.

Your tutor (or adviser, mentor, or supervisor, depending on whether you are on a formal course or in a workplace situation)

You may have more than one tutor. They are on your side, but their job is to challenge you to move your thinking forward (and, hopefully, theirs). You probably know more about your subject area than they do, and they know more about the processes and procedures of research than you, so listen carefully to their advice and act on it. Expect to receive critical feedback as well as praise. If you disagree with your supervisor, stand your ground and argue your case. You are expected to exercise your originality of mind and critical judgement, so go ahead and do so, but be prepared to change your mind in the light of better knowledge. Don't be defensive; the aim is not to score points but to improve practice and advance knowledge – mainly your own – so keep the atmosphere friendly, businesslike and positive. If things go wrong, don't immediately blame your tutor. Assess the situation sensibly and, if it really was your fault, be open about it, look upon it as valuable learning, and start again.

Your fellow action researchers

If you are on a formal course or a professional development programme, you will be one of a group of action researchers. These people are key resources for sharing information on progress and insights, offering feedback, and providing support and challenge. Aim to work collaboratively rather than competitively. You all want to do well. Aim to build an atmosphere of trust and collegiality. This is essential in action research, which is informed by a collaborative ethic.

Your validation group

This group is made up of colleagues, participants, principals and managers, students, and other sympathetic people whom you feel would be able to comment fairly but critically on your research. Look on them as you would someone who is assessing you. They want you to succeed, but they will not accept sloppy research. You do not expect them to be hostile, but you also do not expect them instantly to agree with you. They expect you to justify any claims you make, so do not react negatively to criticism or challenge. It is their job to ensure that your research is valid, authentic and supported by reasonable evidence, and it is your job to learn from the experience and make sure that your work comes up to standard.

Developing ways of working

These people are key resources, and you need to relate to them well. Good interpersonal skills are fundamental to good relationships. Carry out some kind of audit on your own capacity in interpersonal skills. What are your strengths? Are there any areas you need to improve? In particular, aim to develop the following skills.

Listening

Aim to listen more than you talk. If you are not sure how good you are at listening, make a videotape of yourself in conversation, and count the number of times you speak and others speak. Watch the video first by yourself. You may want to share it later with someone such as your critical friend. Aim to say 'you' more often than 'I'. Watch your body language. Being a good listener is far more important, in any walk of life, including research, than being a good talker.

Managing

Managing means managing yourself, not others. Aim to do whatever is required of you to achieve your goals: arrange meetings, carry out assignments, connect with other people. Make sure you attend all meetings, and honour deadlines. Be punctual. Be aware of organisational procedures, and other people's sensitivities. Maintain a professional and businesslike attitude throughout.

Collaborating

Action research demands that you work with others. You are doing your research into your practice, but your practice is about how you are with others, and is carried out in company with others. You need to be intellectually independent, but not an isolationist. Action research is a form of social research; your aim is to help you understand your relationships with others as you try to influence them with educative intent. This does not mean trying to take over their minds. They have a right to their independence and space, as you do to yours. You may want to influence them in ways that you consider educational, but you must be respectful of their opinions. You may aim to challenge but not destroy, and they have the same responsibility to you. Group-think is out, and so is imperialism. This is a pluralist society that tolerates others' opinions and respects their freedom to think as they do. You need to be comfortable with diversity and handle conflict in ways that enable the conversation to continue.

Intrapersonal ways of working

Your most precious resource is you. Personal relaxation and concentration are essential to high performance and a sense of personal fulfilment. Aim to develop a positive attitude. Say to yourself 'I can' rather than 'I can't'. Keep negative experiences in perspective. It is not the end of the world if something goes wrong, more an opportunity to learn and create better futures. Doing research enables you to re-enter the world of learning, a world that many adults forget. Life is a process of constant learning, being in touch with what might be possible and daring to find ways to do it. Professionals often feel anxious that they may not know the correct answers. No one can know everything, and it is exciting to explore this amazing world of ideas.

Inclusive ways of researching

Inclusiveness means including everyone, not excluding anyone. People are different, hold different values and come from different backgrounds. They think in different ways (Belenky *et al.*, 1986), and also learn in different ways (Gardner, 1983). You need to use this understanding to make sense of your life with others. The people with whom you are working may see things differently from you. How do you ensure that all people, regardless of how they are socially positioned in terms of their ethnicity, colour, age, physical and intellectual capacity, sexual orientation or other 'differences', are treated respectfully and fairly? Will you include men as well as women, give as much weight to the voices of adults as of children? Will you report other people's opinions as well as your own? How will you check that you are acting fairly and respectfully throughout? These are difficult issues, but central to ensuring that other people see your research as meeting the demands of social justice. If you can show that you have addressed these issues, you can claim that you are living out the stated goals of your research through its design and implementation.

Style of language

When you present your oral or written accounts, aim to develop an inclusive style of language in speaking and writing that has a clear sense of audience. What people know is what they read or hear. If you want people to understand your ideas, you must express them clearly and unambiguously. Avoid language that is biased towards any group, such as academics or white females. You can expect your audience to be educated, and reasonably familiar with educational enquiry, but you should avoid densely packed ideas and jargon (when you use a specialist term that you understand, but other people might not). Aim to lead your audience easily and without fuss. Do not make great conceptual leaps, or use unnecessarily 'big' words: 'use' is as good as 'utilise'. Equally, do not under-pitch or avoid using a professional tone. Regard your audience as a person whom you are partnering, and walk with them through your work, always checking that they are where you hope they are. It is your responsibility to explain clearly, not theirs to try to work out what is in your mind.

Working with people in organisational and institutional settings

If you are doing a formal action research project you are probably working as a member of an organisation, though not necessarily in an institution. Some published accounts of research in private contexts are available, but they are rare. A lovely example is the story by Christopher McCormack (2002) who undertook his research into his practice at home, but his work was also part of a formal degree course and therefore located in the institutional setting of the university. Most studies are conducted by people who are members of an organisation, and most are conducted within institutional settings.

If you are on an award-bearing course, you are working in two organisational settings: the workplace and the academy. Both carry potential constraints. Be aware of these before you begin your project. If you are not, you could be in for a nasty shock.

Here are some things to look out for.

In the workplace

You are hoping that your work will be supported through appropriate conditions and resources. These come in the form of people, organisational structures and facilities. Here are some aspects you should consider.

People

- Will the people with whom you work support your efforts? Once you have negotiated the base rules (for example, by distributing and receiving back your ethics forms), will you be able to go ahead unhindered? It is essential to get proper clearance and have everything in writing, so that people cannot accuse you later of professional misconduct.
- Will people be available to help you? Will you find sufficient and appropriate people to be your critical friends, research participants, validators? Be realistic here. Many researchers find they have to go outside the workplace to find participants.

- What is the cultural climate like? Are people open to new ideas? Bernie Sullivan conducted her research into teaching Traveller children (Sullivan, 2002), to investigate why they tended to drop out of school early. She found that prejudice permeated the attitudes and structures of the school. When she questioned her colleagues about this she encountered the same kind of prejudice and hostility to herself that had been reserved for the children whom she was teaching. While she could rightly claim to have influenced staff attitudes, and some staff became sympathetic to her work, others changed in the direction of becoming more entrenched and she found herself becoming as marginalised as the Traveller children.
- What is your manager(s) like? Managers tend to set what counts as cultural climates and expectations. Is your manager sympathetic to you? Is he or she interested? Does he or she want to be kept informed, or are they happy to let you get on with it? Does the manager have to report back to superiors? Will there be any problems there? Is the manager open to the idea of professional learning? Is the manager publicly positioned as a learner?

Organisational structures

- Where are you positioned in the structures of the organisation? Do you work in a hierarchical structure where you are directly answerable to a boss? Do you need to check with your boss about your actions and opinions?
- What is your functional role in the organisation? Does it carry specific expectations? Are you expected to conform to established canons? Will your research compromise you in relation to your role? Or are you perhaps in a position to use your power to manipulate existing structures and create new ones to meet your interests?
- What kinds of stories and scripts are used most throughout the organisation? Who says what to whom? How do they say it, and how do they position you? Are you happy to speak the lines someone else has written, or do you want to write your own?
- What will you do if your research reveals injustices, or you come to understand how things have to change? What happens if you then find yourself in conflict with established norms and structures?

Facilities and resources

- Does the organisation commit to the professional learning of its employees? Is time allocated for your study? How about money? Many organisations are willing to fund people's studies, provided that the study can be shown to have significance in the workplace. If not, you may have to fund yourself. You may also have to do your study in your own time. Be aware. While one of the joys of doing action research is that it focuses on the work you are doing, it is bound to take extra time. What will you leave out of your already busy life in order to put the study in?

- Will you be able to use the library if there is one? Will you get financial support for purchase of books? Will you be able to use the workplace photocopier? Who expects to see a copy of your report, and what will happen to it?
- Do censorship practices exist that might prevent you from going public or from speaking your truth?
- If you use organisational facilities and resources, does this have implications for the ownership of your research? Will anyone else claim it as their property? Major dilemmas arise around issues of intellectual property rights, and some end up in court. Be absolutely clear about whose property the research is, and what the conditions are around its production.

In the academy

If you are on an award-bearing course you have chosen, consciously and deliberately, to enter into a legal contractual agreement with an institution. This does not mean you have to conform to expectations, but it does mean that you have to be aware of existing structures and norms, and, if you disagree with them, to work creatively from within. Many published action research reports show how practitioner researchers did challenge academic norms and standards, and created new ones that were then accepted by the academy as legitimate. These are problematic issues that always carry risk. Sometimes it can mean the difference between getting your award or doing things your own way (see Dadds and Hart, 2001: 1–10). You have to weigh up the options and make your own strategic choices.

People sometimes experience difficulty when they assume that their action research will be accepted automatically as a valid form of research that can generate legitimate theory. Donald Schön's famous (1983, 1995) metaphor of the high ground of conceptual theory and the swampy lowlands of practical knowledge still holds true for today, though, thanks to the efforts of thousands of action researchers, the situation is changing. Previously, only theoretical conceptual knowledge was regarded as 'true' and worthwhile. Now, personal practical knowledge is also acknowledged as true and worthwhile. The practical embodied theories of practitioners are now accepted as legitimate knowledge.

Where you are positioned institutionally will depend on what precedents have been set at your institution through previously validated work. Some institutions, such as the University of Bath and the University of the West of England, have impressive databases of action research dissertations and theses, and these now constitute new canons. If you are in an institution such as these, few problems are likely to arise. If you are in an institution that has no established or emergent tradition of new scholarship work, you will have to draw on other knowledge bases to locate and support your efforts (see e.g. http://www.actionresearch.net and http://kml2carnegiefoundation.org/kml/login/).

Your tutor is your best support. If they are experienced they will be politically aware and strategically shrewd, and will guide you expertly. If they are relatively inexperienced, they will count as much on your support as you on theirs, to achieve their aims of changing the knowledge base at their institution and the structures which communicate that knowledge.

Possible implications

Persistence is an important quality, but by now you are possibly wondering whether it is all worthwhile, and if you should press on regardless. The answer is, Yes, you should, in spite of the potential hazards involved. The world needs you, and many more like you. If you remain silent and inactive, injustice will prevail, and defenceless people will go under. If you do decide to take action, be strategic and do the following.

Find allies and join networks

You cannot do it alone. Allies can offer support and comfort, propose alternative strategies, and help you check whether your thinking is right.

Maintain high standards of scholarship

Make sure your work is academically rigorous, and will be accepted on all counts mentioned in Chapter 1. The more practitioner research is validated by the academy, the more it will be regarded as valid knowledge, and the more it will strengthen public opinion. Your work must always demonstrate integrity, accuracy and coherent thinking, so that it cannot be faulted on technical grounds.

Publish

Aim to publish your research wherever possible. Having work published is one of the highest markers of academic and organisational worth. Aim to build up a track record of publication so that you have a platform to speak from.

Work at all levels of the system

In organisational contexts, work at all levels of the system. Aim to talk with everyone, including senior and middle managers. You cannot afford to privilege any one section; otherwise you could alienate others and build a new kind of prejudice into the structures.

Support others

You have much to contribute, and others will benefit from your insights. Remember that this is all about learning, and we learn with and from others. Be generous.

Always keep a clear sense of what is possible, and let that act as your driver as you encounter what is structurally not possible. Your vision of good is stronger than life's constraints.

Chapter 4

Influence and ethics

Every time we say or do something, we are potentially influencing someone somewhere. No one is ever isolated, even though we might think we are. We are always connected with others in space and time through our creations and our ideas. This carries significant implications for what we say and how we act.

This chapter deals with influence and its educative potentials, and also explains the kinds of checks and balances that are necessary for ensuring, as far as possible, that influence is educative. It deals with the following issues:

- What is meant by 'educative influence'?
- How can an awareness of ethical issues help to ensure that the influence will be educative?
- How do you justify your influence?

Educative influence

It is often assumed that influence is negative and sinister. This is not necessarily so. Influence happens in many ways. It is also often assumed that one person can directly influence another. Again, this is not necessarily so. People mediate other people's influence through their own originality of mind and critical judgement. Coercion aside, people have choices about whether or not to be influenced. When we speak about educative influence, we imply that this involves a process in which person A comes to help person B understand that A is helping B to make choices about whether or not B should accept A's influence. This is not a crude, coercive process. It is highly complex, and means establishing contexts in which freedom and originality of mind are safeguarded for all by all. Too often it is the case, however, that some people persuade others not to exercise their choices. For many, choices really do not exist. Others are not even aware that they have choices.

The type of influence we exercise therefore depends on how we act. We can influence in ways that are educative; that is, aim to help people learn and grow in freedom, as well as in ways that are destructive. The idea that our potentials for influence are embodied in the way we act implies that influence is in the quality of our relationships. If those relationships are educative and grounded in commitments to freedom for all to learn and grow, the influence will probably also be educative.

There are no guarantees, however. It is possible to be false in relationships, pretending sincerity, in order to manipulate others and get one's own way. Play-acting at educative relationships reduces the potential for educative influence. The influence itself may be described as educative; it may be anything but.

These are problematic issues that continue to occupy the energy of many philosophers of education. It is a central issue for this book. In doing action research, we are aiming to improve our practice. Our practice means our work with other people. Our work always involves relationships. In one sense it could be said that our work *is* our relationships. Each one of us potentially is in a position of power, because we always have the possibility of influence in someone else's life. In doing our research, we purposively aim to influence other people's lives in an educative way; that is, to help them to learn and grow through freedom of spirit and body.

Therefore, rigorous checks and balances need to be in place to ensure that our work is having the educative influence we intend, and that we can recognise the other's educational responses when these responses differ from the ones we had hoped for. These checks and balances take many forms. One form is validation processes, which are outlined in Chapter 9. Another important check is demonstrating ethical awareness, and this is yet another problematic area. Demonstrating awareness of ethical practice is not the same as acting in an ethical way. It is possible to know the theory but not to implement it for various reasons. Researchers are often faced with dilemmas; for example, does it make sense to produce ethics statements for people who have difficulty in comprehending? Specialist books are available that explain how to deal with these dilemmas, and to find ways of conducting ethical research, but there are few concrete answers.

This book, we hope, is informed by ethical awareness. We also hope the ideas expressed here demonstrate our sense of what is right in terms of other people's welfare. You need to make your own decisions about your actions and contexts. You also need to accept the responsibility of your actions. This is an awesome undertaking.

One of the first places to begin is to understand and implement the ethical principles of action research processes.

The ethical principles of action research processes

You must have a good grasp of the ethical considerations of action research. Colin Robson (1993) reproduces the guidelines on the ethical principles for conducting research with human participants from the British Psychological Association, as well as summarising the work of Kemmis and McTaggart (1982) about the ethical principles of action research. Other sets of ethical guidelines may be obtained from organisations such as the British Educational Research Association and the American Psychological Association. However, action research processes involve more than simply conducting research with human participants. Action researchers aim to influence human participants.

Action research, as outlined in this book, is a process of self-study. New work is appearing specifically in relation to practitioners' self-study (see Bullough and Pinnegar, 2001; Zeni, 2001). The field needs to be developed. It is important not only to talk about the principles involved, but actually to demonstrate how practitioners and writers act in a way that aims to influence others in an ethical manner.

Checklist of ethical considerations

Here is a basic checklist of ethical considerations. It is not comprehensive, nor does it cover all contingencies. As your research progresses, always check with others that you are fulfilling your ethical commitments.

Draw up your documentation

You need to prepare and distribute ethics documents to all participants. Your documents should include an ethics statement and letters of permission. If you are writing an account of your project, include blank copies of this documentation in your appendices, and make sure you conceal all the names of people or organisations. In letters of permission, check that you have blanked out names, addresses and signatures.

Your documentation will include the following.

An ethics statement

This is your personal statement about how you are going to conduct your research, and should mention all the points below in some way. Make copies of this statement before you begin your research, and give everyone a copy as they become involved. Your statement should include room for your and their signatures; you and they should keep identical copies for your files. Do not be embarrassed at giving these documents even to close friends and colleagues. It is part of good research practice.

Letters of permission

Draw up letters of permission for all participants. As above, make copies of these letters and distribute them to people as they become involved. Always make sure they and you have identical, signed copies, and store your copy carefully. We live in an age of litigation. If anyone has difficulty reading, give them a letter but also explain things orally, and do so again at regular intervals. In your letters, say when the data about themselves will be destroyed, and make sure you honour your commitments.

At the end of this chapter you will find exemplars of an ethics statement, and letters to principals and parents. You can adapt these to suit your own purposes. The principles and values involved travel to most contexts.

Negotiate access

With authorities

Check with principals and managers before undertaking research that is connected with their (your) organisation. Establish boundaries about what you may and may not do. Obtain this agreement in writing. Be absolutely honest about what you plan to do. If your plans change during the course of the project, let the principal or manager know, and get their permission to proceed.

With participants

Obtain permission from the people whom you hope to involve in your research. Keep them informed. Invite them to do their own action research. Make it clear from the start that they are participants and co-researchers, and not 'subjects' whom you are studying. You are studying yourself, in relation with them. Explain this carefully, and as many times as necessary for them to become comfortable around what you are doing. They are key resources; handle them with care.

With parents, guardians and supervisors

If you are working with children or other people who are under supervision, make sure you obtain permission from parents or other supervisors to involve those people in your research. Send a letter home, explaining what you are doing, or arrange an information meeting. If anyone is experiencing reading difficulties, explain things orally. Get people on your side from the start, and keep faith with them.

Promise confidentiality

Confidentiality of information

Give a firm undertaking that you will report only that information which is in the public domain and within the law. You will not reveal anything of a personal or compromising nature. If you wish to use information that is in any way sensitive, seek and obtain permission from the originator to use it.

Confidentiality of identity

Do not reveal the real names of people or places unless you have specific permission to do so in writing. Do not give people fictitious names; those names may belong to other people elsewhere. Allocate initials, numbers or other symbols to identify participants. If the organisation gives full written permission to use its real name (and many organisations are delighted to do this), go ahead, but you must obtain written permission first.

Confidentiality of data

If you wish to use firsthand data such as transcripts, or excerpts from video recordings, always check that this is acceptable to the originators and obtain their written permission. Check that your perceptions of the data are accurate. Always ask the originator to check and approve transcripts, and edit their contribution as they wish. Encourage others to read your versions of events before you publish them.

Ensure participants' rights to withdraw from the research

You must check continually to make sure that participants are comfortable with procedures and are always in full command of their own involvement in your research. You must let your participants know their rights are protected, that they may withdraw if they wish, and that all data about them will be destroyed at a time you negotiate with them.

Ensure good professional and academic conduct

When you gather your data and produce your report, make sure that your practice is academically and professionally sound. When in a lecture or group setting, do not tape-record anything without permission. When interviewing people, make sure that you explain how the data will be used, and stick to your commitment. When you write your report, always acknowledge your intellectual debts, and do not use other people's words without acknowledgement. Do not expect your tutor to provide references, or to read your drafts umpteen times. Doing research is a professional practice that requires commitment to hard work and personal responsibility.

Keep good faith

Establish right from the start that you are a person to be trusted, and that you will keep your promises about negotiation, confidentiality and reporting. Never take anything for granted. Always check back with people if there is any doubt, and, in matters where there is some possibility of misunderstanding, write down what you are hoping to do and get that approved. While you have a duty to protect others, you also need to protect yourself.

At the end of the day, having observed all these issues, and demonstrated your integrity and authenticity, keep faith with yourself, and go ahead and publish your work. Claim your work as your intellectual property, and be aware that you are contributing to a body of knowledge that is of worth in the world.

Justifying your influence

Nothing in human relationships comes with guarantees. In your action research you are acting in a way that you hope will lead to learning and growth, and your validation processes will help you check whether you are fulfilling that aim (Chapter 9). You cannot guarantee this. Producing documentation about ethical issues is part of the story, not the whole story. By taking care in ethical conduct you are hoping to make reasonably sure that you will act in a way that minimises potentially harmful consequences, and even that is often not possible.

Perhaps the main issue is to maintain your own integrity in accordance with your own values. If you stay true to your values of what contributes to others' benefit, and make every effort to show how you are doing this, you can fall back on your integrity as your main justification. We are justified when we act with honesty in the direction of the welfare of the other. Perhaps this is where our educative influence can be strongest, when we show, through the way we live our lives, that we acted honestly out of a sense of others' best interests, and out of a sense that they have the capacity to make their own choices. Our decisions may turn out to be the wrong ones, based on wrong assumptions, and we have to put our mistakes right if at all possible. Often it is simply not possible, and that is something we have to live with. But the foundation of personal integrity and honesty in action is a wonderful coat that action researchers wear. This coat cannot be bought. It is something we make for ourselves, created out of our own experience, and therefore to be cherished all the more.

Examples of ethics statements

Your ethics statement can be simple or complex, depending on what you wish to achieve. A simple ethics statement is:

ETHICS STATEMENT

I, [name], promise to ensure good ethical practice in conducting my research. I promise at all times to negotiate permission to conduct the research, respect confidentiality, and ensure participants' rights to withdraw at any time from the research.

[Your signature] ....

[Your name]

A more complex statement is:

ETHICS STATEMENT

Dear [name],

I am undertaking an action research project to study my own practice as a [type of work]. This ethics statement is to assure you that I will observe good ethical practice throughout the research.

continued on next page

This means that:

- the permission of my Principal and Board of Management will be secured before the research commences;
- the permission of the children and their written consent will be secured before the research commences;
- confidentiality will be observed at all times, and no names will be revealed of the school, children or staff;
- participants will be kept informed of progress at all times;
- participants will have access to the research report before it is published;
- I will report only that which is in the public domain and within the Law;
- all participants have the right to withdraw from the research at any time and all data relating to them will be destroyed.

[Your signature] ....

[Your name]

Examples of letters requesting permission to do your research

Example letter to parents

[Your institutional address]

[date]

[Name and address of parent]

Dear [name],

Permission to undertake research

As part of my work with the [organisation, or name of project], I am conducting a piece of action research into studying how I can encourage children to improve their word skills using computers. I would be grateful if you would give your permission for [name of child] to take part.

continued on next page

My data collection methods will include audio and videotape recordings of the children and myself in conversation, photographs, diary recordings, field notes and reports. I guarantee that I will observe good ethical conduct throughout. I promise that I will not reveal the name of the school, colleagues, parents or children at any time, unless you inform me in writing that you wish me to do so. If you wish I will keep you informed of progress throughout. My research report will be available at school [work] for scrutiny before it is published.

I would be grateful if you would sign and return the slip below at your earliest convenience.

I enclose two copies of this letter. Please retain one copy for your files.

Yours sincerely,

[Your signature] ....

[Your name]

✂ -

To [your name],

I, [name], give my permission for [child's name] to take part in your research.

[Parent's signature] ....

[Parent's name]

Example letter to Principal

[Your institutional address]

[date]

[Name and address of Principal]

Dear [name],

Permission to undertake research

As part of my work [with name of project where appropriate], I am conducting a piece of action research into studying how I can encourage children to improve their word skills using computers. I would be grateful if you would give your permission and support for this project.

My data collection methods will include audio and videotape recordings of the children and myself in conversation, photographs, diary recordings, field notes and reports. I guarantee that I will observe good ethical conduct throughout. I will negotiate permission to work with the children. I will secure permission from parents and children to involve them in the research. I guarantee confidentiality of information and promise that no names of school, colleagues or children will be made public without your permission and the permission of those who wish to be named.

I promise that I will make my research report available to you for scrutiny before it is published, if you wish, and I will make a copy of the report available for your files on its publication.

I would be grateful if you would sign and return the slip below at your earliest convenience.

continued on next page

I enclose two copies of this letter. Please retain one copy for your files.

Yours sincerely,

[Your signature] ....

[Your name]

✂ -

To whom it may concern

I, [name], Principal of [name of school], give my permission for [your name] to undertake her/his research in her/his classroom and in the school.

[Principal's signature] ....

[Principal's name]

Chapter 5

Action planning

Now you can begin your action planning. As a first step, it is helpful to think through some of the underpinning concepts that provide frameworks for the research. These are often called 'conceptual frameworks'. Look back at Chapter 2. The concepts outlined there now begin to come to life through the planning processes described in this chapter.

Some frameworks

Action research involves a continuous process of acting, reflecting on the action, and then acting again in the light of what you have found. Many people think of it as a cycle of action–reflection. When the work appears as an ongoing process, it can be seen as a cycle of cycles.

A useful starting point for thinking about the action–reflection process is as follows:

- We review our current practice;
- identify an aspect we want to improve;
- imagine a way forward;
- try it out;
- and take stock of what happens.
- We modify our plan in the light of what we have found, and continue with the 'action';
- evaluate the modified action;
- and reconsider the position in the light of the evaluation.

So far, this is a basic problem-solving procedure. Different action researchers have described it using a variety of verbal and visual models. Some present it as cycles of reflective action (Lewin, 1946; Griffiths, 1990); some as flow charts (Elliott, 1991; Evans, 1993a); some as spirals (Kemmis and McTaggart, 1982; McNiff with Whitehead, 2002). The most useful models represent the idea of practice as non-linear, showing that people are unpredictable and creative, and that life seldom follows a straightforward path.

However, action research is not only a problem-solving procedure, although it involves a problem-solving procedure. Action research is about identifying what we want to achieve in terms of the values we hold, and offering justification for the actions we take, and this is more than problem solving. In this light, the basic problem-solving procedure becomes less simple than it first appears. For example, how do we identify an aspect that we want to improve, and why do we want to improve it? Although action research is not necessarily about 'problems', and may start from the point where we are simply interested in something and want to follow it through systematically, action research always involves a sense of tension that inspires us to take action, even if the tension is a sense of wonder.

Experiencing oneself as a living contradiction

Jack Whitehead understands the incentive for beginning a personal study to come from experiencing oneself as a 'living contradiction'; that is, feeling dissonance when we are not acting in accordance with our values and beliefs. For example, we may say that we believe all children should speak for themselves, yet we often find ourselves in family, classroom or workplace situations where we actively prevent children from speaking for themselves. Jack has expressed his ideas as follows:

- I experience a concern when some of my educational values are denied in my practice;
- I imagine a solution to that concern;
- I act in the direction of the imagined solution;
- I evaluate the outcome of the solution;
- I modify my practice, plans and ideas in the light of the evaluation.

(Whitehead, 1985, 1993)

The 'I' exists as a living contradiction in the sense that values are denied in practice. It is often not easy to see ourselves as living contradictions. We use all sorts of defences or excuses to hide from ourselves the realisation that we may not be living in the direction of our values.

When we begin our action research, we usually conduct what many writers term a 'reconnaissance phase'; that is, when we begin to clarify for ourselves what is going on that makes us want to get involved. The first steps in action research processes are often tentative and muddled, and the initial data we collect is often less convincing than the data we collect later in the research. As we continue, however, reconnaissance turns into proper action planning, with clearer intentions and envisaged outcomes, and the research becomes more systematic.

Action planning

A good starting point is to consider some key questions that will form the basis of your action plan. The questions are presented below, and they are followed by the kind of ideas and issues that will help you address them. Try to paraphrase the answers to see if they may be applied to your situation. Create your own answers, or change the questions. This way you can begin to generate your own personal approach to doing action research. Always aim to create questions and answers that suit your own working context and personal values position. A word of warning, though. Action research, like all research, is about finding out something we don't already know. It is not an excuse to confirm prejudices, so make sure you develop your capacity for listening and understanding other points of view, and try to find alternative explanations to challenge your own point of view. In this way you can make your position more explicit and argue a clearer case for practices that enable you to live your values more openly.

Some key questions for action planning

- What is your research interest (or issue, or concern)?
- Why have you chosen this issue?
- What kind of evidence can you produce to show what is happening?
- What will you do about what you find?
- What kind of evidence can you produce to show that what you are doing is having an impact?
- How will you evaluate that impact?
- How will you ensure that any judgements you may make are reasonably fair and accurate?
- How will you modify your practice in the light of your evaluation?

The action plan in detail

Here are some provisional responses to the questions. Check if they fit your situation. If not, make up your own.

What is your research interest?

Ask yourself, 'What issue do I have to deal with in my personal professional life?' Your answer may be broad or narrow in focus. Perhaps you need to manage your time better, or help a particular person, or change an element of a curriculum, or develop your capacity for listening, or restructure your organisation for more sustainable working practices . . . or a thousand other issues. It is important to focus on one issue only as your research programme, among all the other issues of daily practice. You may find that this one issue is symptomatic of other aspects of practice. It can take time to focus. At first you may feel overwhelmed by the whole situation, but a focus tends to emerge through reflection and conversation with others.

The research interest may be expressed as 'What is my concern?' What you wish to investigate may be a concern, or even a problem, though not necessarily. You may want to undertake an evaluation of current practice. However, this would probably be only the beginning of your research. You would go on to find ways of ensuring that the situation remained satisfactory or was changed appropriately. The main point is to identify an area that you want to investigate, and be reasonably sure that you can do something about it.

You and your research

Remember that you are the focus of the research. You are investigating your work with others. You are not investigating them. That is for them to do. You are hoping to influence them so that they come to see how they can learn how to deal with their own situations and lives. You are researching the extent to which you are helping them to do this. Although you are investigating 'a situation', the 'situation' is made up of yourself and others; you and they constitute the situation. You are asking, 'How do I change this situation by helping others to think and act for themselves?', and you keep records of what you do as you respond to your own question.

Beginning from where you are

All research begins with a latent hypothesis. Traditional social scientific hypotheses work on a cause and effect basis, and take the form, 'If I do this, such and such will happen'. Action research hypotheses are not so much hypotheses as working hunches, and take the form, 'I wonder what would happen if . . .'. This means that action research begins from where people are and takes real-world situations as the area of interest.

Having identified your research issue you now need to formulate it as a research question. Action research questions are generally expressed as 'How can I . . . ?' or 'How do I . . . ?' or 'What can I do . . . ?' You should also be practical and ask, 'Can I actually do something about this issue? Can I hope to influence the situation, or am I out of my depth?' Be realistic. You cannot change the world, but you can influence your part of it. For example, you may want to investigate reductions of funding for the adult education service in your community. You can do nothing on a large scale because it is probably connected with the wider political-economic situation. However, you could mobilise the adult learners in your institution to lobby the local policy makers to present their views about the importance of adult learning. This is a small step that could contribute to a better understanding by politicians. You would express your research issue as 'I am concerned that the level of funding for adult education is falling', and your research question could be 'What can I do to raise the level of funding?' If you and others share the same research intent, you could ask, 'How do we raise the level of funding?'

Here are some more examples:

- 'How can I persuade management to introduce new consultation procedures in this organisation?'
- 'How do I help A to improve her self-confidence?'
- 'How will I manage my work schedule better?'
- 'How do we evaluate whether our student care programmes are working for the benefit of the students?'

Central ideas

- I am the central person in my research. I am investigating how I can help others to learn to make their own choices.
- I am asking a real question about a real issue, and I am hoping to imagine a possible solution.
- I am starting from where I am. I am starting small and focusing on a local issue with wider intent.
- I am trying to influence the situation towards improvement. Remember, any improvement is still improvement, no matter how small.
- I always remember that 'the situation' is not an abstract entity, but comprises real people. Consequently, I am not trying to improve 'a situation' so much as trying to help people to help themselves.

Why have you chosen this issue?

You need to be reasonably clear why you want to get involved in this area. Action researchers hold a value commitment to improving the quality of life for themselves and others. Be aware of your own values position, although this can be very difficult. We live in social contexts, so we already hold certain values which influence our actions and the way we judge other people's actions. Our thinking is already conditioned. We try to live by our values, but how do we show that our values are justified? This is a difficult question which is developed on page 144.

Because we already hold values, we often experience ourselves as living contradictions. A teacher, for example, may believe that his students should speak for themselves, yet prevent them from speaking. A manager may say she believes in collaborative working, but then not involve others in decision making. These are examples of how we may deny our values in practice by behaving in an unreflective way. An aim of action research is to develop reflective practices so that we are clearer about our own motives.

Sometimes institutional issues present constraints. A doctor may want to pay more attention to the people in her care, but, given her workload and bureaucratic pressures, there simply isn't time to do so. A community leader may want to accommodate more people, but policy and financial considerations restrict numbers (see Chapter 10 for further discussion).

No one can solve broad issues on their own, but they can take steps towards improvement. Mountains are climbed one step at a time. It is always possible to reach the top, even if it means taking different pathways, trying out different strategies, and resting frequently. Often it means working as a team, with one person picking up where another left off. Action research is a way of working that helps us identify the things we believe in and then work systematically and collaboratively, one step at a time, to making them come true.

What kind of evidence can you produce to show what is happening?

- How can other people see your particular situation through your eyes?
- How can you show things as they are now, before you begin to take action?

Gathering data and producing evidence

Data refer to the information we collect about a situation. These data transform into evidence when the data are checked against working criteria and their relationship to those criteria is established. The process happens like this.

Turning data into evidence

1   You gather data using a variety of techniques (see pages 114–128).
    You sort the data into categories.

2   You begin to articulate criteria by which you believe the validity of
    your research can be established. For example:

    • If your aim is to encourage greater participation in the work-
      place, a criterion could be whether people do begin to partici-
      pate more.
    • If your aim is to encourage others' independent thinking, a
      criterion could be whether previously passive persons begin
      to voice their own opinion.
    • If your aim is to help unemployed people develop confidence
      to help them get a job, a criterion could be whether their
      improved confidence did help them get the job.

3   You generate evidence by searching the data archive and finding
    instances that relate to the criteria. For example:

    • Your January fieldnotes tell how Mr A and Ms B did not
      participate very much in workplace social events. Your June
      fieldnotes record how those two people organised a team-
      building exercise.
    • In a tape-recorded conversation with your study groups, Ms B's
      voice is not heard. In another recording six weeks later, she is
      heard to challenge someone's opinion and voice her own.
    • A letter from now-employed Ms J thanks you for helping her
      develop her self-confidence which has enabled her to get a
      new job.

4   From the data you extract specific pieces that you feel support or
    refute your belief:

    • 'Mr A and Ms B undertook to organise the team-building
      exercises' (fieldnotes, 6.6.02).
    • 'I am not sure I agree with you. I think democracy should be by
      the people as much as for the people' (Ms B, tape-recorded
      conversation, 10.8.02).
    • 'I got the job mainly because I felt much better about myself,
      thanks to your support' (extract from letter received from Ms J,
      8.9.02).

continued on next page

These pieces of data can now stand as evidence, because they are related to a claim to know. The data does not change its form. It changes its status. The words and images remain words and images, but they now take on the status of evidence because they are specific instances that you feel are especially relevant in showing the validity of your research (see page 14).

NB: It is important to remember that evidence can confound as well as confirm our expectations. Sometimes the evidence reveals that things are not going according to plan, or that what you may believe is successful is not viewed in the same way by others. You need to stay alert to this possibility, and take appropriate action according to what the evidence reveals.

When you begin your project you may not be sure about which data to gather. You may need to gather a lot of data before your main issue emerges. It can be difficult to decide which data to use for particular purposes. Aim to gather your data and store them in one place, such as a cardboard box. As you progress, sort the data into categories, and do this regularly. Put data about different aspects into their own boxes, and keep a separate box for odds and ends. The data you collect become part of your research archive. Over time you will probably rethink your categories, and that will mean sorting and allocating your data in different ways.

Gather data according to what you want to show. For example, you could identify a small group of people who would show a particular behaviour. If you were evaluating a particular programme, you may work with different participants over time. You could select, say, three people from any group of twenty, and ask them to keep records of their progress over time. You would keep your own records. You do not have to capture every action or every word spoken, only those you feel are representative of the whole.

Which participants? Which data? Which criteria?

Now you have some specific decisions to make in response to the questions 'Which participants?' 'Which data?' 'Which criteria?'

Which participants?

You probably work with many people. Your wider work goes on; your research focuses on one small aspect of that work. It is impossible to research every aspect even of this narrowed field, so you need to be selective. Identify a small group of people as your research participants. These people are representative of your wider work. Be reasonably sure that they will help you to generate the kind of data which will enable you to make judgements about your developing work together.

Don't feel pressured into choosing a large group. It is perfectly feasible to do a piece of quality action research working with one person (see e.g. Holley, 1997). The focus of your work is you, and you are your main source of data. Your research participants are sources of data that show how you are trying to exercise your educative influence. Perhaps they will also begin researching their work, and you would become a source of data for them. Always negotiate access and permission with your participants; don't take anything for granted.

Which data?

You are the main focus of your research. You are not trying to show a cause and effect relationship between you and others in the sense of 'If I do X, they will do Y'. You are trying to show an improvement in your practice. The evidence for this lies in the extent to which you are having an educative influence on others. They need to say whether or not you are influencing them in ways that help them to learn. It might be argued that they will agree with you, just to please you (or perhaps because they are afraid of you). How can you avoid this? You can never avoid it entirely, but you can produce reasonable evidence to show that you are acting with honesty for their benefit. This evidence may be found in any data that shows you in interaction with others in ways that improve their learning. You could rightly regard this kind of data as sufficient. However, you would have a much stronger case if you and your participants were to look at your data together, and comment separately on how you had influenced the quality of each other's learning. You would record these comments as further data. You and your participants would share records of practice, negotiate your perceptions, and come to a collective agreement about your findings. These processes provide strong sources of data to show how you are holding yourselves individually and collectively accountable for your work.

Which criteria?

You need to identify criteria and standards of judgement for you and others to judge whether you are achieving your goals. Your criteria will be related to your values. If your values include ideas that people should think for themselves and make their own decisions, your criteria will be whether people do think for themselves and make their own decisions. Your values, which you hold at a tacit level, become your living criteria when they emerge within your practice. If you can show that you have enabled people to think for themselves and make their own decisions, you can say that you are living your values and meeting your criteria.

To do this you need to pull out of the data any instances that you feel show people thinking for themselves and making their own decisions. These episodes show the fulfilment of your criteria. Ideally you should aim to gather your data in relation to the criteria you have identified. You may use paper documentation, such as letters, diaries, and your own fieldnotes, or audio and visual documentation, such as audio and video-tape recordings. However, it may take time to develop your criteria: they may emerge only as you work your way through the data. Be clear from the start about how important it is to develop criteria, and this will guide you as you gather your data with an eye to turning it into evidence.

When you start producing evidence from the data, the data itself will not change. You will select pieces from the data, and those pieces will change their status, because now you are matching the data with your criteria, and turning the data into evidence. This is very important when you come to make your claim to knowledge, because claims always need to be backed up by evidence, not data, and evidence is always understood as in relation to nominated criteria.

What will you do about what you find?

First, you should question your own interpretation of your data. Imagine different ways in which it could be interpreted, and talk with others about what you could do. Remember that any decisions for action should be your decisions, not other people's. It is also your responsibility to ensure that whatever you decide to do remains focused and manageable, and does not involve organisational upheaval for others.

Having decided on a possible strategy, try it out. It may work or it may not. If it does work, continue developing it. If it doesn't, try something else.

Many researchers feel that if they don't immediately 'solve' an issue, or if they don't achieve an anticipated 'result', they have failed. This is not so. Things do not often work out as anticipated. Nor can you 'change' situations, other than in relation to changing yourself and trying to influence others to change themselves. Change happens in people's minds, and this mental change then transforms into actions. Look on your project as an opportunity to develop your own thinking and practice as you try to influence others. If you can show that you have developed your own thinking and have learned, that is enough. Your improved thinking is an outcome of your research. Clearly, your claim to knowledge is much more robust if you can show that your improved thinking has helped others to learn. Be clear about what you are claiming, and produce appropriate evidence to support your claim.

In your report, you need to show the process of the development of your own and others' learning. Evidence for this will be found in your collective records of practice. Try to show the possibly chaotic and punctuated processes of learning: how the unexpected happened, how you came to see that issues that you believed existed only at a surface level were in fact symptomatic of underlying matters. Studying your own communication skills may reveal that you fidget or don't look people in the eye. Or perhaps you put people down in subtle ways. A concern such as 'How do I improve the way in which people of mixed race are perceived in this organisation?' could show that there is structural prejudice throughout the organisation. This kind of 'explosion' is common. Stay focused, and remember that this is a small-scale project. You may come to regard it as the first cycle of a project that develops into several progressive or developmental cycles. It may also be the first cycle in what will become a larger project, or an ongoing feature of your everyday work. Whatever the overall shape of your project, stay focused on the issue you have identified for this stage.

What kind of evidence can you produce to show that what you are doing is having an impact?

Aim to gather data on a regular basis. Keep records of how you are monitoring and evaluating each cycle. These become your case records and show the developmental nature of your work. It is not quite the same as 'before' and 'after' data, because you should be able to show a progression of events that include your own changing understandings of the situation and a re-evaluation of the position you held at the beginning of the research.

For example, Eileen Brennan (1994) wanted to investigate how she could improve her practice of teaching German to a poorly motivated first-year class. She followed through a number of action–reflection cycles, tackling separate issues one at a time: first, an over-emphasis on writing; second, how to present the material in a stimulating way; third, a focus on improving the accuracy of written work; and fourth, a concentration on vocabulary building. For all these activities she kept a research diary, and gathered substantial data which she transformed into clear evidence. She writes:

> At the beginning of the school year I found my class so undisciplined and unmotivated that I was driven to giving them lots of written

work to keep them quiet and busy. This went against my values as a language teacher. As a preliminary to deciding what I could do to remedy the situation, I discussed with them their experience of the German class to date. Subsequently I asked them to write me a letter telling me why they had chosen to learn German and what they hoped to do with it.

On the basis of their comments . . . I devised strategies to make the learning process attractive and fulfilling for the class. These included tapes, role-playing in pairs, reading advertising materials (we exchange materials with a partner school), playing language-based games, singing German songs and writing to pen-pals in Austria and Germany.

I believe I can show, from videotapes, audiotapes, oral and written tests, written work and questionnaires, that discipline has considerably improved and that together, my pupils and I have developed a class environment conducive to language learning in a relaxed and enjoyable mode, and yet productive of the standards required by the Junior Certificate syllabus.

(Brennan, 1994: 54)

Monitoring the research and generating data are technical activities that should improve as your research goes on. Aim to triangulate the data; that is, obtain data from more than one source to use as evidence to support a particular explanation, and show how the data from these different sources all go towards supporting the explanations you give of your situation. This is important in getting other people to validate your claims to knowledge. Your claims could be seen as subjective claims, even as your opinion. Purely subjective explanations that lack supporting evidence do not give other people confidence to take them seriously, or to try out similar practices for themselves, so they are not very useful. It is important to show how the findings from your research can be useful for other people, because action research is about learning to improve quality.

Your report becomes part of an emerging literature containing people's stories of how they have improved their practice. This literature is part of the knowledge base that is helping to strengthen the legitimacy of practitioner-based research.

How will you evaluate that impact?

The focus of your research project is you, and how you judge the quality of your educative influence on other people. To repeat: this is not a cause and effect relationship. You are not saying, 'These changes are happening because I did such and such.' You are saying, 'I can show that certain changes took place, particularly in myself, and different relationships evolved.' Critics may say, 'How do you know that these changes wouldn't have happened without you?' Your answer would be, 'I don't, but I do know that they are happening with me.' You cannot be held responsible for what may or may not have been, but you are responsible for influencing others, so you need to make sure that your influence is the best it can be.

In evaluating your research and establishing its potential worth, you need to show what has improved, and how. The whole of your action research is an evaluation process, because you:

- gather data;
- identify criteria for improvement;
- select pieces of data to act as evidence of improvement;
- match the evidence with your initial research concern;
- present your work for others to judge whether or not there is improvement.

An individual practitioner cannot make a final judgement about his or her effectiveness in relation to the educational development of another. The outcomes of the research are in the lives of yourself and others. If lives are better, the research may be evaluated as worthwhile. Only participants themselves may say what they mean by 'better'. The negotiation of values is a fundamental part of educational action research.

This is why it is very important to secure firsthand data from other people, and to be careful about using it as evidence. For every piece of evidence, make sure that you include information about dates, places and people who were present. Your data need to be authenticated, so aim to get signatures on documents and transcripts, show the authorisation for the use of data, and obtain authentication from, say, critical friends for your fieldnotes. These kinds of verification procedure show your responsibility as a researcher.

How will you ensure that any judgements you may make are reasonably fair and accurate?

If you say, 'I think such and such has happened', you can expect someone to say, 'Prove it'. While you can't 'prove it', it is important to produce reasonable evidence to suggest that what you feel has happened really has happened, and you are not just making it up. This is not the same as 'proving it'. You are aiming to show how you have done things differently, and to comment on the value of the changes.

To say that things are now better is a bold claim, and it is not enough simply to assert the claim. Other people need to agree that you have done what you claim to have done, and that it now counts as 'better'. To do this, they need to agree what counts as good in the first place. Ideas about 'good' are related to people's values base. For example, judging how patient care may be improved involves asking what constitutes good patient care. Does it involve patient information control or patient compliance? From what we agree to be good practice, how do we judge whether the work is better now than it was in the past, and how do we test that out?

A notional procedure therefore has to be agreed, something along these lines: You and I agree what counts as good practice. I present my work to you. I identify specific criteria and I produce evidence. You scrutinise my work. You agree that I have improved certain aspects, or you ask me to revise my ideas. If I trust your judgement I will make the revisions, and resubmit my case. We then test our collective judgement by putting my work and our discussions into the public domain, and see if they are taken up by others.

This kind of critical testing and validation is essential. We establish the value of our work against the stringent checks of significant others to be reasonably sure that we have something of worth.

How will you modify your practice in the light of your evaluation?

If your new way of working appears to be more in line with your educational values and visions, continue with it, but don't stop the evaluation process. If the new way does not seem to be working, try something else.

You may not be entirely satisfied with your practice, although you have made progress. You will probably never reach perfection, because as soon as one issue has been addressed, other issues seem to arise in its place. We live with the paradox of the ideal: we imagine the way things could be, but as soon as we have an answer, new questions arise. Your present thinking is your best thinking yet, but you know it is going to develop, as it has already developed, and improved. Each day you have is the best, and tomorrow will be even better. Life is always dynamic and changing, even to the moment we die. It is what we do with that life that counts.

This is what makes an action research approach such a powerful methodology for personal and social renewal. We are thinking and searching all the time. We are never complacent or content to let things be as they are, not from any sense of dissatisfaction, but simply from a sense that life does change, we change and others change. Nothing stands still. If we once accept that we have arrived, we rest and fall asleep. As long as we are aware, alert, constantly open to all our new beginnings, we will continue to become more than we are. But it is not only ensuring personal renewal that most of us seek as professionals. Particularly in education, we are also seeking social transformation so that we have a significant impact on institutions and society to create a better context in which we and our children can have better opportunities to learn and to grow.

Part III contains checklists for action, built around the questions that form the basis of this action plan.

Part III

Getting ready for action

Part III gives practical advice and checklists for getting started on your project. Remember: these are guidelines only.

HEALTH WARNING

When things are written like this, they appear to give the impression that doing action research is neat and tidy. It is anything but! This kind of analysis helps in making sense of what we are doing, but in reality we usually find that a project does not fall into neat sections as it appears on the printed page. There is a lot of overlap, retracing of steps, review, redirection and refocusing. The process tends to be zigzag rather than sequential. You need to stay on task in what may appear initially to be chaos. Your tutor and critical colleagues can be helpful supports. They can keep you focused, and help you to make sense of your work. Many people experience turmoil and instability when they first start doing their research, and often things do not fall into place until the project is well under way. Keep on, have faith!

Chapter 6

Getting ready for action

Before you begin, draw up a provisional forward planner to give you a rough idea of what needs to be done (for an example, see below). This planner is for a sixteen- to twenty-week project. You can adapt it to your own needs.

Example of a forward planner

SCHEDULE FOR ACTION RESEARCH PROJECT

Your name ....

Task undertaken   *weeks*

Preparation

    Identification of research area   1–3
    Initial reading   1–5
    Ethics statement drawn up   1–5

Resourcing

    Budget drawn up   1–3
    Budget submitted: request for funding   1–3

continued on next page

Working with other people

Discussions with management and policy makers	1–2
Invitations to potential groups of participants	3–5
Invitations to critical friend(s)	2–5
Invitations to potential validation group	3–5
Letters requesting permission sent out	3–5

Doing the project

Identification of concern	3–5
Gathering of data (first round)	3–5
Identification of working criteria	3–5
Imagined solutions	5–7
Implementing the solutions	5–12
Gathering data (second and further rounds)	5–12
Generating evidence (matching data with criteria)	10–12
Convening validation group	13

Writing up the report   13–16

Evaluating the project   13–16

You will probably draw up a more detailed planner than this. You would identify critical friends and groups of participants. The more thought you put in at this stage, the more successful your project is likely to be. In addition, if you give this kind of information to managers and principals, they will be more likely to endorse your plans. Time spent in planning is well invested.

Beginning on the next page you will find useful checklists for your action plan. Use them to help you keep track of progress. Aim to develop them for your own situation. The boxes will help you check what has been done, and what still remains to be done.

The checklists are organised broadly under the following headings:

- Getting started
- Doing the project
- Evaluating
- Modifying
- Writing up

This section is useful for first-time action researchers. If you are more experienced, go to Part IV on page 97.

Getting started

Finding a research interest

What aspect of your work are you going to investigate?

Have you: *Yes!*   *When?*

- Identified an area you wish to investigate?   ☐   ....

- Related it to your work?   ☐   ....

- Kept it small, focused and manageable?   ☐   ....

- Considered whether you are reasonably confident
  that you will be able to show an improvement in
  your practice?   ☐   ....

- Considered whether you are reasonably confident
  that you will be able to show an improvement in
  your situation?   ☐   ....

- Begun to think about a research question
  ('How do I . . .')?   ☐   ....

- Anything else?   ☐   ....

Tips

Aim to complete the question 'How do I/we improve . . .' as the starting
point for your research. Don't worry if you can't formulate your question
precisely. Researchers tend to have an idea about what they want to
investigate and the idea begins to take shape as new insights develop
through action and reflection. This can take a long time, and sometimes
a new question, or several new questions, will emerge. Stay with one
question only; shelve the others for later attention. You may decide to
abandon your original question and go for a new one.

Tasks

In your working file, write out:

The area you hope to investigate. Put this in terms of your question, 'How
do I improve . . .?' Show how this is related to your work. Give a brief outline of the context. Say how you are hopeful that you can influence your
situation in some way.

Background reading

Have you: Yes!   When?

- Read enough subject literature to give you a
  reasonable foundation?   ☐   ....

- Read enough methodology literature to give you a
  reasonable foundation?   ☐   ....

- Kept a working notebook with key ideas and authors? ☐   ....

- Kept an index file with references – author, title,
  date, place of publication, publisher?   ☐   ....

- Identified which books and papers you still need
  to read?   ☐   ....

- Identified where you will get them?   ☐   ....

- Identified who can advise?   ☐   ....

- Anything else?   ☐   ....

Tips

- Ask your tutor (if you have one) for reading lists to guide you.
- Use the library. Ask the librarian for advice on conducting literature searches.
- Find out the necessary computer databases and abstracting and indexing services.
- Buy essential texts for yourself.
- Don't feel you have to read a book cover to cover. Be selective.
- Access Internet resources for further contacts and examples of validated reports.

Tasks

- Read actively. Keep notes as you read.
- Write on your own books if you wish. Never deface library books.
- Keep a computer database or a card index system of books and papers. File them under author's name, or title. How you organise them is up to you, but stay consistent. Put down key sentences from the work as you read, and always include the page number.
- Use your database to build up your references in a systematic way. When you write up you must get your references accurate. Do not ignore this warning!
- Keep a file of important photocopied papers. Respect copyright laws.

Ethics

Have you negotiated access with, and obtained
permission from: *Yes!*   *When?*

- Principals/managers/others in authority?   ☐   ....

- Your research participants?   ☐   ....

- Parents/supervisors?   ☐   ....

- Colleagues?   ☐   ....

- Others? Who?   ☐   ....

- Have you produced your own ethics statement and
  distributed it?   ☐   ....

- Anything else?   ☐   ....

Tips

- Never skip this stage. You may find you cannot complete your project if
  you do not have the necessary permissions.
- Read the ethics statements of other people to get an idea of how to write
  one.
- Seek advice if you are unsure of any aspects. Better safe than sorry.

Tasks

- Write out your ethics statement and give a copy with every letter
  requesting access. Write letters of permission well in advance.
- Keep all letters in a file to show that you have negotiated issues of
  access and confidentiality as part of your database. Have ready blank
  copies for your appendices. You can later refer to your letters to
  show that you were serious about ethical issues, and if anyone queries
  permissions.

Resourcing

Have you:	Yes!	When?
• Planned the budget for your project?	☐	....
• Secured the necessary funding?	☐	....
• Catered on a shortfall of funds, and allowed a safety margin?	☐	....
• Considered aspects such as printing and other logistical factors?	☐	....
• Checked that all necessary technology is available?	☐	....
• Negotiated its use with others?	☐	....
• Worked out a time-line for your project?	☐	....
• Anything else?	☐	....

Tips

- If you are looking for funding you will need to apply well in advance. Make sure that you have budgeted for the duration of your project. There is little worse than running out of money!
- Obtain quotations from reputable typists/printers well in advance. Check the availability of reproduction facilities.
- If you do all your own typing, get a good computer. Most come with word-processing software. Make sure it has Internet access. Learn to type using all your fingers. Touch-typing is quite easy and an invaluable lifelong skill.

Tasks

- Draw up as detailed a budget as possible. Aim to stick to it.
- Keep a file of correspondence to do with finance.
- Keep a monthly record of accounts. This can be time-consuming, but it is essential.

Working with others

Have you: Yes!   When?

- Established a working plan with your tutor?   ☐   ....

- Identified your critical friend(s)?   ☐   ....

- Agreed a schedule and plan with them?   ☐   ....

- Established who your research participants will be?   ☐   ....

- Talked through your ideas with your participants?   ☐   ....

- Identified your validation group and agreed a
  schedule of meetings with them?   ☐   ....

- Anything else?   ☐   ....

Tips

- Aim to do most of this in advance, although some aspects can be done as the project develops. Never assume that people will do what you want them to do. Ask in advance. Like you, they have busy diaries.
- Aim to keep your participants involved by producing regular mini-reports.
- You must produce formal progress reports for your supervisor and your validation group, to let them see how your project is developing and how you are systematically achieving your overall aims (or not).
- At the end of the project, send a copy of the final report to members of the group out of courtesy, and thank them for their involvement. It is the least you can do – remember, you may need them later!

Tasks

- Negotiate a working plan with your tutor and write it down. This is your responsibility, not your tutor's. Give them a copy, and refer to it throughout the duration of the project.
- Once you have identified all your participants, write to them inviting them to be part of your research. Let them know what will be involved; for example, how many meetings, what their responsibilities are. Negotiate times, dates and venues with them.

- For your validation group, draw up a schedule of meetings. The number of meetings will depend on the length and duration of the project. Aim to meet at critical points in your research, such as when you are presenting the data, or outlining a turning point in your research (this means having a research schedule yourself that you are working to).
- Produce regular progress reports and send them in advance of any validation meetings. Draw up a list of key questions you would like your group to answer.
- Keep all these records in your data archive.

Doing the project

Identification of concern

Have you: *Yes!*   *When?*

- Identified an area that you can do something about?   ☐   ....

- Discussed it with your tutor?   ☐   ....

- Discussed it with other colleagues?   ☐   ....

- Ensured that it is an area of practice in which you
  can probably show improvement?   ☐   ....

- Identified how the situation is not in keeping with
  your educational values?   ☐   ....

- Anything else?   ☐   ....

Tips

- Check with your tutor that this is a reasonable research area.
- When you do your preliminary reading, choose one or two keywords and check who else is doing research in your area. Perhaps no one else is, or there may be some valuable research you can draw on. It is important to keep up with your field.
- Check whether key policy recommendations exist around this area. Will your research contribute to new policy? How?

Tasks

- Begin to formulate your research question in terms of 'How do I . . .?'
- Write down a brief description of your context to show why you are concerned, and how you hope you may be able to improve things. Consider personal, locational, research and policy contexts; that is, who you are, where you work, what research exists in the area, and what policy recommendations are relevant to your work.

Values statement

Have you: *Yes!*   *When?*

- Identified the values you hold as a professional that
  are possibly being denied in this situation?   ☐   ....

- Imagined what the situation would be like if it were
  in keeping with your values?   ☐   ....

- Considered what it would take to bring the situation
  into line with your values?   ☐   ....

- Checked your own perception of what is happening?
  Are you justified in intervening in this situation?   ☐   ....

- Made a record of your values statement for future
  reference?   ☐   ....

- Anything else?   ☐   ....

Tips

- Think about why you have chosen this particular area. What are your
  professional values, the motives that drive you to do the job you do?
- To what extent are you working in the way you wish? What do you need
  to do in order to improve the situation?
- Can you reasonably justify your planned intervention in this situation
  for educational reasons?

Tasks

- Write out your professional, educational and social values. You could
  write this in terms of your personal mission statement.
- Give a brief description of your work situation, and say whether you are
  living in the direction of your values.
- Say why you feel you are justified in intervening in the area you have
  identified. If possible, show that you have checked your perception
  with someone else. You are not just interfering; you really do have a
  reasonable foundation for your intervention.

Gathering the data (first round)

Have you:	Yes!	When?
• Decided what kind of data you can gather?	☐	....
• Decided on possible data-gathering methods and instruments?	☐	....
• Decided on initial categories for the data?	☐	....
• Made sure that any necessary technology is available?	☐	....
• Discussed with others the kinds of criteria you could use to judge the effectiveness of your action?	☐	....
• Anything else?	☐	....

Tips

Gathering data

- There is always a temptation to gather any and all data. Be careful. You should identify key areas that will help you to show that you are improving your situation.
- Remember that data is not evidence.
- Keep data boxes. If you are gathering data for several different areas, use different coloured files or boxes, and put all your pieces of data into these boxes.
- Never throw away any data until the project is finished, and even then be selective (remember to destroy any data according to what you have negotiated with participants).
- Make a list of the possible data-gathering techniques you could use, and number them in order of preference. This will help you identify what you would be most comfortable with. Choose from the techniques out-lined in Chapter 8.
- You can mix and match all these techniques. However, don't feel you have to use them all, and certainly not all at once.

Storing data

- Don't anticipate that technology will be readily available. Check before-hand. Make sure you liaise with other colleagues about use of technology.

- If you are keeping your data on computer, make back-up copies of information, and back-ups of back-ups. We have all experienced losing material due to failure of technology. Save your work at frequent intervals.

Ethics

Always obtain permission before you do any taping or distribute question-naires. If people refuse permission, you must not go ahead. Respect ethics and sensitivities.

Evidence

Discuss with colleagues what kinds of criteria may help you make judge-ments about progress. Discuss with them what may count as valid evi-dence.

Tasks

- Identify the group you are going to work with. Ask and obtain group members' permission before you begin your project.
- Choose your data-gathering methods and instruments. Make sure that the necessary hardware is available. Negotiate its use with colleagues.
- Identify and write down your initial categories for the data. Put this information on your data files or boxes. Use sticky labels or other devices that can be changed (you may need to change your categories as the project develops).
- Set about gathering the data, and put it into your data files or boxes.
- Keep in touch with your tutor and other colleagues at this stage. Obtain their feedback on what you are doing, and let them see your categories and data. Work out with them the criteria that are going to help you generate evidence.
- Imagine what the evidence may look like.

Imagining possible solutions

Have you: *Yes!   When?*

- Imagined at least one possible solution to your
  concerns?   ☐   ....

- Written down ideas for other possible solutions?   ☐   ....

- Planned a systematic strategy for implementing the
  solution?   ☐   ....

- Checked with colleagues that your action plan will
  not interfere with their schedules?   ☐   ....

- Invited them to talk through ideas?   ☐   ....

- Anything else?   ☐   ....

Tips

- Think about possible action plans. Think in terms of 'Plan A, provided (x) and (y)', or 'Plan B, if (a) and (b)'.
- Imagine possible future scenarios. What will be happening in two months' time (or your preferred time-line)? How will it be different?

Tasks

- Write down your possible solutions, in response to your general question, 'What can I do about this?'
- Make these possible solutions available to any of your participating groups that may help at this stage. Ask their advice. Ask them for their possible solutions.
- Draw up a route map to get to this situation. Brainstorm ideas with colleagues. Draw up diagrams and visuals about possible maps and strategies.
- Check with colleagues that your plans will not cut across theirs. Remember good ethical conduct.

Gathering the data (second and further rounds)

Have you: *Yes!*   *When?*

- Decided on the kind of data you hope to collect for
  your second round?   ☐   ....

- Decided on data-gathering methods and instruments?   ☐   ....

- Decided on categories for your data?   ☐   ....

- Decided on the criteria you are going to use to
  generate evidence of improvement?   ☐   ....

- Identified the types of critical incident that are going
  to show the criteria in action?   ☐   ....

- Talked through your ideas with critical colleagues
  and friends?   ☐   ....

- Anything else?   ☐   ....

Tips

- This is your second set of data. You may gather further sets of data later.
  You can use the same methods and instruments that you used for the
  first round, or different ones.
- You may want to have a second set of colour-coded files or boxes to
  compare the first round of data with the second. If you go on to
  gather further sets of data you may want to get more boxes, or, preferably, begin to reorganise your data into existing or new categories.

Tasks

- In the same way as for the first round, allocate data to different files or
  boxes. Focus on the criteria you feel provide clear evidence to show
  that you have improved your situation in some way. Discuss these
  with critical colleagues. Write them down.
- Ask colleagues how they would judge the changes in your practice, as
  well as in that of your participants. If possible, tape-record some of
  these conversations. When you go through the transcript, highlight
  those pieces of the conversation that could be real instances that show
  progress. These pieces will constitute your evidence. The rest of the
  transcript can go into the data archive.

Evaluating

Evaluating the impact of your project and its significance

Have you: *Yes!*   *When?*

- Identified criteria that you believe will show where
  change is happening?   ☐   ....

- Highlighted critical incidents in your practice which
  show how improvement is happening (or not)?   ☐   ....

- Pulled these incidents out of the data, and shared
  them with critical colleagues and friends?   ☐   ....

- Anything else?   ☐   ....

Tips

- This is the time when you begin to generate evidence from the data.
- Keep the following questions in mind: How can you show the development of your own learning? How can you show that things are happening with you? How can you show that you really are influencing people
  so that they are changing their practices? Who will endorse what you
  are saying? What will be your key pieces of evidence?
- Also keep in mind: Does the evidence show that events are going in
  ways contrary to what you anticipated? What do you need to do?
- Use a mental highlighter pen to pick out those significant pieces that
  constitute clear evidence of change. Keep a record of these significant
  pieces as you work through your project.

Tasks

- Decide what counts as evidence, and think about how you can present it.
- Extracting from your data, write out any critical incidents so far that will
  meet your criteria.
- If the data reveal that things are not going according to plan, write down
  how you need to adjust your thinking and practice.
- Pay particular attention to transcript material. This can be powerful,
  particularly if you ask participants to reflect on the process of your
  work together, and invite them to say whether or not they feel that

the situation has improved. A few pertinent lines of transcript is all you need. Place the full transcript in your archive for the time being; this may appear in your report as an appendix.

- Begin to compile a systematic record of evidence. Build up an 'evidence box'. This can be any container that will take your various pieces of critical data. Make sure each piece is dated and coded to show where it features in the time-line of your project.

Validating the claim to improvement

Have you: *Yes!*   *When?*

- Identified your validating group, and organised a
  schedule of meetings with them?   ☐   ....

- Organised your data so that you can produce clear
  evidence to support your claim that you have
  improved your practice?   ☐   ....

- Identified possible criteria by which that claim
  can be established?   ☐   ....

- Considered other possible criteria?   ☐   ....

- Anything else?   ☐   ....

Tips

Now you are aiming to present evidence to support your claim to knowledge, and you are going to ask people to agree or suggest modifications.

Important questions to ask

What are you going to claim to have achieved? What improvement do you
think has taken place? How are you going to justify your claim? By what
criteria do you want your work to be judged? Who will set those criteria?
Will you be able to negotiate the criteria? What data will you select as
evidence to meet the criteria? Will you include data that will possibly
refute your claims?

Tasks

- Organise your evidence. Collate your data so that you can identify and
  show what you think you have achieved.
- Extract critical incidents that you feel act as evidence. Say how you
  believe these to show improvement. Say how you feel justified in
  making your claims.
- Arrange a meeting of your validation group. Send them a progress
  report, referring to your evidence.
- At the meeting, invite your validating group to offer feedback.
- Listen, and resolve to act on their advice.
- Record the meeting, in writing or on tape, and put the record in your
  data archive.

Modifying

Modification of practice

Have you: Yes!   When?

- Reflected on the feedback from the validation group?   ☐   ....

- Considered whether your new form of practice is
  more in harmony with your values?   ☐   ....

- Imagined ways in which you can share your new
  insights with others?   ☐   ....

- Imagined ways in which this may be of benefit to
  your organisation, and shared those ideas with
  others?   ☐   ....

- Identified aspects of your new practice that need
  attention?   ☐   ....

- Anything else?   ☐   ....

Tips

Now you are moving into the final phases of the project and will shortly publish your findings. Check with significant others if this is still all right. Renegotiate, if necessary, anything they may question.

Tasks

- Write down how your practice has changed.
- Reflect on the responses from your validation group, and aim to incorporate them into your verbal and written reports.
- Arrange discussions with any significant others before writing up your report. Ask them to comment on how your work may impact upon the organisation.

Evaluation of the experience of doing the project

Have you: *Yes!*   *When?*

- Considered what doing the project has meant for
  your own learning?   ☐   ....

- Considered how your learning may influence others?   ☐   ....

- Asked the opinions of your research participants?   ☐   ....

- Asked the opinions of others in your organisation?   ☐   ....

- Considered how you may have done things
  differently?   ☐   ....

- Considered how you may do things differently in
  the future?   ☐   ....

- Anything else?   ☐   ....

Tips

- It is important to consider two aspects of your learning: (1) what you
  learned about the area you were researching; (2) what you learned
  about yourself while you were doing the project.
- Was it worthwhile? How can others learn from your experience? You
  need to make these issues explicit when you write the report.

Tasks

- Write out how the experience of doing the project helped you to understand your own practice (and yourself) better.
- Write out how you think you influenced others in an educational way.
- Reflect on the responses of others, and consider how you will incorporate these into your report.
- Think about what you have learned, both about the subject area, and
  also about your own learning.
- Say how you intend to share your learning, so that others can learn from
  you.

Writing up

Have you:	Yes!	When?
• Set aside enough time to get the project written up?	☐	....
• Organised a writing schedule?	☐	....
• Arranged for typing if the work is going out?	☐	....
• Arranged for binding and other reprographics?	☐	....
• Organised your work folders, disks, index boxes and data archives so that you can access material quickly?	☐	....
• Anything else?	☐	....

Tips

People approach writing tasks in different ways. Some are highly disciplined, putting in so many hours per day. Others go on inspiration, working when they are in the mood.

- Decide what is your own preferred style. Be honest, though.
- Don't put off writing up. It can take a long time, and you don't want to rush at the last minute.
- If you find writing difficult, tell your story, possibly to a friend or to yourself, using a tape-recorder. Talk it through, and then transcribe the talk.
- Explore with your tutor if there are ways other than (possibly as well as) writing that you can use to present your work. Would the examiners accept videos instead of, or as well as, a written report?
- Organise any material to go into your appendices.

Tasks

- Organise a work schedule. Write it down, and put it in a place so that the family can see when and where you will be working. Be ruthless about your time (well, almost ruthless).
- Arrange your workstation so that it is friendly. Have everything you need to hand.
- Write up the report along the lines of Chapter 12

- Expect to draft and redraft several (possibly many) times. First drafts tend to be wordy. Each time focus down, until you have a concise, professional document.
- Think in terms of who gets a copy of the work, and how you can distribute it (or pieces of it) more widely. Also consider how you may submit if for publication in a journal.

And finally . . .

This now marks the completion of your first action reflection cycle. You have come full circle, but you have not closed the circle. You have moved beyond, and are now ready to undertake another action reflection cycle.

If you feel that the way you are now working is better than before, you will probably stay with this new way of working. However, there is probably still room for improvement, or perhaps new aspects have emerged that you need to address. You can say with justification that you have improved an aspect of your practice, and this can be a tremendous incentive for further action.

Part IV

Doing your project

The quality of your research ultimately depends on the quality of your evidence. You are hoping to make an original claim to knowledge, and you will support that claim with unambiguous evidence. Your evidence is generated by identifying success criteria that will act as key indicators for judging the validity of your research, and then drawing out from your data instances which show the criteria in action (page 64). Your evidence is already in the data. The quality of your evidence depends on the quality of the data you collect.

Collecting and organising the data involves the same processes of action and reflection as the rest of your project. You are active in gathering the data, and then you reflect on what you have gathered in order to arrange it so that the actions it represents begin to make sense. In the same way that your project is a transformative process of realising values as practice, so also is your data collection and organisation a transformative process of turning raw data into meaning.

Part IV gives advice on how to collect and organise data. Chapter 7 advises on how to monitor and document the action, and Chapter 8 shows you how to deal with the data so that it begins to take coherent and meaningful shape.

Chapter 7

Monitoring and documenting the action

This chapter gives advice on monitoring the action and documenting the processes of action research. It contains the following sections:

- How to monitor and document your action research: general principles
- Gathering data and looking for evidence
- How to manage the data: general principles
- How to involve other people in the monitoring process

How to monitor and document your action research: general principles

Your action is at the centre of your action research. It is not just any kind of action, but action to which you, the researcher, are *committed* by your personal and professional values, action that is *informed* by your careful considerations about its appropriateness, and action that is *intentional* and undertaken by you to achieve the goals you have set. Monitoring the action should help you to meet these high principles.

Collecting, interpreting and evaluating your data

Monitoring the action is more complicated than simply collecting data about how you perform an aspect of your work. It involves three distinct operations:

1 collecting data about the action so that it documents the clearest possible description of what has happened;

2   interpreting the data you have collected so that you can develop a
    tentative explanation of what has happened;
3   evaluating what you have done so that you can re-plan for further
    action.

Monitoring the action means generating data to use as a basis to reflect on
and evaluate what has happened, and to plan further action. This constitutes the action–reflection cycle (see page 58).

How may you generate data?

Some of the action will be your own personal action, and some will be
other people's. Generating data therefore involves:

- monitoring your own action;
- monitoring other people's action;
- possibly monitoring critical conversations about the research.

Let us imagine you are a teacher mentor and you are working with a
newly qualified teacher (for an excellent discussion about mentoring see
Fletcher, 2000, and http://www.teacherresearch.net). You are observing
the teacher's lesson. Your own research question is, 'How can I improve
the feedback I give to the teacher before and after the lesson?' Any
answer to your question will involve generating data by monitoring your
own action as you provide feedback, monitoring the teacher's lesson
before and after the feedback session, and possibly monitoring your discussion of this sequence with a critical friend.

Monitoring your own action

To monitor your own action you need to identify your intentions and
motives before the event and your subsequent reflections, as well as
what you actually did. You may record your intentions and motives in
your research diary, together with your plans for the session.

    You could generate data about your action by audio or videotaping the
feedback session or by making notes yourself and asking the teacher to
make notes. You could be more formal and ask a colleague to observe
the session using one of the observation techniques discussed on
pp. 118–121. You could ask the teacher to complete a short questionnaire
about what happened, or interview them subsequently. This will provide
you with data about your action from various perspectives (triangulation).

    The next task will be to make sense of your data so that you can evalu-
ate the action. Evaluation is part of the monitoring process. Making sense
of the data and testing out your interpretations will mean that you need to

involve other people such as your critical friend or other colleagues from your workplace or elsewhere.

Monitoring other people's action

In the example we are using, this would involve monitoring the teacher's lessons before and after the feedback session. This raises an important issue.

Action research is not about making judgements for other people. It is more about making judgements about yourself and the quality of your educative influence, by inviting them to make judgements about themselves. You are not trying to change them; you are helping them to make the right choices about how they will re-create themselves. You would invite people to document their own practice for two reasons: (1) so that they can make judgements about their own work, and (2) so that you can use their documentation to show your educative influence by explaining, interpreting and evaluating your interactions with them. They would provide data for your research, and you would provide data for theirs. You and they would be researching your individual practices collaboratively. Your questions could transform from 'How do I . . .?' to 'How do we . . .?'

In the example, you could:

- ask the teacher to record their intentions and motives as well as provide a formal lesson plan before the lesson;
- videotape the lesson, as well as make notes yourself and ask the teacher to make notes;
- discuss the data with the teacher and together arrive at interpretations that are acceptable to both.

Monitoring critical conversations about the research

Critical conversations about the research should take place at all stages of the process. 'Critical' does not imply negative criticism. It refers to the process of critique, when we problematise issues and unpack them for hidden meanings and assumptions. In the example, there are three obvious places for you to engage in critical conversations with the teacher and others:

- you could talk about your plans and intentions;
- you could share your data about the action;
- you could invite criticism of your interpretations and evaluations and your subsequent plans.

It is important to document the critical conversations that occur at all these points. Recording such conversations:

- celebrates and records significant moments of change in practice (yours and others');
- enables you and others to show changes in your thinking over time;
- provides information that the validation process has been continuous and formative.

It is important to ensure that you are encouraging others to become co-researchers who contribute a critical perspective that informs your research; otherwise they may become mere respondents who supply answers to questions you have framed. This will not move you beyond your present way of seeing things. Their contributions to your project will help you show that they are active participants and not simply providers of data.

Data, evidence and audience

Monitoring the action should provide you with data about the action that, when analysed and evaluated, may be used as evidence to support your claims about what you have learned as a result of the research (see Chapter 9). Remember that data is not evidence. Data becomes evidence when it is used to support a claim in relation to specific criteria, in your case, how the values that led you to do the research became more of a reality in practice.

Records can also provide you with the raw material from which to write reports and articles about your research (see Chapter 12). The different audiences for whom you write will require different types of descriptive material. You need to take this into consideration when you are planning how to monitor and document your action research. This is particularly so when providing data to support the different kinds of claim you will make about it.

For example, suppose your action research has been in response to the question, 'How do I improve my practice as Head of the Maths Department?' As a result of your enquiry you are able to claim that students are doing better at mathematics. You may have to produce evidence for the following people:

- Your principal or director may want evidence that your research has influenced specific outcomes such as improved examination results. In this case you could provide test data, based on before and after results. However, you should not think that action research processes must 'bring about' concrete outcomes. Unfortunately, some action researchers do adopt this view (see Introduction), and this can lead to frustration for participants when things do not go according to plan. We authors believe that an 'outcome' in terms of personal learning is as valid as statistically demonstrable 'results'.

- Other colleagues may want evidence of the processes. For example, you may have led a departmental team that had developed ways of working which made the curriculum more student-centred. To show this you could produce evidence of changing teacher–student interactions. Video recordings could show this.
- If you are involved on an award-bearing programme you may be asked to support claims that you have learned from the research process. You could present evidence of personal reflection and learning perhaps from your diary and taped conversations with relevant others.

A number of different tasks are involved in monitoring the action, but you have a great deal of choice in how you carry out these tasks and which techniques you use to generate data. Always draw where possible on your own expertise and experience. Remember also that most data-gathering techniques (qualitative and quantitative) can be incorporated into action research.

Gathering data and looking for evidence

Remember that your action research is about you, in company with other people. You are looking for evidence to show how you have improved the quality of your work in order to enhance the quality of their experience. Evidence about your actions exists in data generated about you. Evidence about the quality of your influence exists in data generated about others. You can judge the quality of your work as an action researcher by the extent to which other people begin to think and act in a way that is in harmony with your educational values; that is, they live lives that are characterised by freedom, justice, truth and beauty.

Remember that evidence can confound as well as confirm your expectations (see p. 65). If the evidence shows that you are not having the educative impact you had hoped for, you need to revise your thinking and develop alternative action plans.

Bearing this in mind, think of the instances and places where you can find your evidence. At each stage in your action plan, think in advance about which sources of data may yield evidence. Use the following ideas to help you.

What is your research interest?

Look for evidence in the data, for example:

- journal in which you recorded your initial thinking;
- tape-recorded conversation and transcript when you discussed the situation with your colleagues;
- note of complaint to your manager, pointing out that a particular issue needed addressing. Letter from your manager in reply, suggesting that you do something about it first.
- Other?

Why are you interested in this area?

Look for evidence in the data, for example:

- audio/videotape-recorded conversation with colleague and transcript, talking through the values you hold that make you want to undertake the investigation;
- letter to a friend, saying that you want to get involved because . . .;
- informal written report, commenting on how much you have enjoyed reading a novel that spells out exactly what you are feeling in regard to your situation.
- Other?

How will you establish what the situation is like?

Look for evidence in the data, for example:

- questionnaire to colleagues to get their reactions to the current situation;
- invitation to students/workplace colleagues asking them to comment on their perception of the current situation (remember that this will involve your performance, which means that they may well critique you);
- video-recording of current situation (again, be prepared to face up to reality when you view the video. View it alone first, and then invite a sympathetic colleague to view it with you).
- Other?

What can you do?

Look for evidence in the data, for example:

- written action plans about how you may tackle the matter;
- journal to show how you gave it thought and imagined possible strategies;
- illustrations of your own, showing possible future scenarios once you had intervened in your practice.
- Other?

What kind of evidence can you gather to show that what you are doing is having an impact?

Look for evidence in the data, for example:

- second questionnaire asking participants to comment on how the situation may have changed and if it is better;
- video-recorded group discussion of how the situation may be better;
- letters from parents commenting on the difference in participants' attitudes at home.
- Other?

How will you explain that impact?

Look for evidence in the data, for example:

- audio/videotape-recorded conversation with validation group in which specific criteria and categories were discussed;
- journal to show reflection on categories and criteria;
- fieldnotes from participants referring to group discussion when categories and criteria were discussed.
- Other?

How can you be sure that the judgements you have arrived at are reasonably fair and accurate?

Look for evidence in the data, for example:

- audio/videotape-recorded conversations and transcripts with validation group on viewing data from critical incidents;
- written feedback from validation group to say that they agree that you have done what you claim to have done (they are now validating your claim to knowledge). Alternatively, suggesting other things you could have done, or ways in which you could improve on what you have done;
- written feedback from participants to say that they agree with your report (again, this is validation of your claim to knowledge).
- Other?

These are only examples. You can probably find evidence in any or all data sources if you look. The sources mentioned above are not exhaustive. Be imaginative, and find ways yourself of showing which data can generate quality evidence.

How to manage the data: general principles

To manage your data efficiently, you need to consider your working materials, how you are going to categorise and store your data for easy retrieval, and how you are going to use the data.

Your working materials

You will need:

- one or several working files;
- data boxes;
- a computer (ideally);
- an index box and cards if you haven't got a computer, optional if you have;
- a journal;
- key books;
- your own work space if possible;
- several small notebooks.

Your working file holds all your rough jottings and materials that you may need at a later stage. This is an active file. You are constantly putting in and taking out material.

Your data boxes hold all your pieces of sorted data. Use several coloured or otherwise identifiable boxes such as box files or copy-paper boxes. Cereal boxes are good. Label each box with the categories for your data, such as 'conversations' or 'fieldnotes'. You may change your categories as you proceed. For example, the general label 'conversations' may become 'conversations with colleagues' and 'conversations with participants', in which case you would sort the separate categories into their own files. Put your pieces of data into their appropriate boxes. These boxes begin to constitute your data archive.

Your computer is an excellent investment, and will take over many jobs that previously involved sorting and categorising, including the compilation of databases, references and indexes. Don't worry if you cannot manage the software. Index boxes and cards are just as good.

Index boxes and cards are ideal for keeping records of relevant books and articles. Always write the title of the book or article, together with author, publisher, place of publication and date. For articles from journals, record also the page numbers from the article. If you find an important quotation, write this on your card together with the page number where it appears. Keep your references from the start. When you write up the report, you must get your references right. Remember that it takes ages to find a missing reference, particularly if the book is back in the library.

Your journal (or diary, or log) acts as a record of events, and also a record of your thinking about those events. You can use a notebook or a loose-leaf file as your journal. This can also act as a piece of evidence, to show how your actions and thinking changed over time. Aim to write up your journal regularly. You don't need to do this every day, but you should set a pattern for yourself and stick to it. You can find detailed advice on diary keeping in Chapter 8.

Key texts will act as constant sources of reference. If you have access to a library, use the resources there to help you locate the texts. If you find some books are essential as key texts, buy them. Never deface library books. Regard your texts as good friends with whom you are having an ongoing interesting conversation.

Your own work space is important. Good lighting, space and ventilation are desirable. Good equipment is helpful but not essential. Your own computer and printer will save you hours of time and a lot of money in the long run. Other people, such as family, should not invade your space when you are using it. Put a note on the table as a reminder. If you are sharing a space, arrange with your partner when you can each have access.

Small notebooks are handy. Important ideas hit us at any time. If you have a notebook with you whenever possible, you can jot down the idea. Leave your notebooks in key places in the home, at work, in your pocket. You never know when inspiration will strike. Get into the habit of writing things down, and this itself generates more ideas.

Finally . . .

Yourself. The most important thing is your own sense of well-being. Sometimes the best thinking is done at unplanned times, and the best writing is done on the backs of envelopes, on a bus, in the middle of the night. If you feel good about yourself, your work will be good. All the equipment in the world cannot substitute for your own sense that you have something worthwhile to contribute. Be sure that you have, and enjoy your project.

Managing the data

Your data emerges as a result of monitoring your action as you work your way through your action research cycle. In this way, data begins to emerge as your records of plans and actions, and the steps you took to reflect upon and evaluate these as you created them. Try to be systematic in managing these records efficiently. Organise and index your data regularly. It does not matter which system you adopt, as long as you are consistent.

The management of data is rather like the organisation of memory, consisting of three parts: storage, (en)coding and retrieval.

- *Storage* refers to the system of organising the data in a physical space;
- *Coding* refers to the process of sorting and labelling the data;
- *Retrieval* refers to the methods used to pull it out of the store and using it in a meaningful way.

Storage

It is not useful to place all the data willy-nilly into one large box and label it 'my archive'. You should aim to store your data in terms of the forms and sources in which it exists.

Data can take a variety of forms that include:

- conversations
- pictures and other visuals
- notes
- thoughts and ideas

Locations for these types of data include:

- video- and audio-tapes
- children's work
- documents
- texts – fieldnotes, diaries, completed questionnaires
- computer disks
- record cards

It is up to you to decide how to categorise your data and store it in terms of these categories. You may find that your categories change over time, and you should aim to resort your data when necessary.

Coding

Coding involves labelling and sorting.

Labelling

Each item of data should be labelled so that you know what it is. Your label should indicate:

- when it happened
- where it happened
- what it was about
- who was involved
- any other information that you consider important

Sorting

There are two main ways of sorting, which can also be cross-referenced:

- Types of data distinguished in terms of the **chronology** of the project; that is, data generated at different stages of an action research cycle or from different cycles of action that have occurred over time.
- Types of data about different **aspects** of the project such as library research, reflective self-study, workplace contexts, a staff room context, conversations with critical friends.

You may find that different files or colour-coded boxes are helpful.

Sorting the data can provide an archive of case records that may be used as primary source material (Stenhouse, 1978: 36). This case record is a comprehensive account of what you have done. A major criterion, as Stenhouse noted, is that the record should be accessible for critical scrutiny by others. Therefore, when you are preparing your data archive, remember that it is not only for your information but also for other people to see. You are familiar with your material; they are not. When you present your research report, you will have to lead people carefully through the records of your actions, so always organise and present your work with this in mind.

Retrieval

You will need to retrieve your data and present it in order to provide evidence for the claims that you make about the research. Much of this data can be large; for example, physical videotapes or diaries or portfolios of practice. Stenhouse (1978) recognised that much of the data in an archive was too bulky and detailed to present to others, and therefore he argued that the archive should have two aspects: the case data and the case records.

- **The case data** are all the materials you have assembled. These constitute your archive. When you write your report, you would refer to this archive, but you would produce it only if required. Some limited aspects may go into the report as appendices.
- **The case records** are what Stenhouse called 'a parsimonious condensation of the case data' or 'an edited primary source'. This means that, in the body of your report, you would insert extracts from your data to support a specific point. You would include other data that provide a context for your extract in your appendices.

Consequently, your data will appear in different forms in your final report:

- in the main body of the text, as extracts to support a specific point;
- in your appendices, as immediate contexts for the extracts, or as elaboration of the specific points you are making;
- in your archive, as the more general material from which you have extracted your data.

A reminder that, when planning the compilation and contents of your data archive, always bear in mind the ethics of using data that involves other people (see Chapter 2). Have you cleared everything with your participants? Have you got their approval to use their real words? Are individual identities well hidden?

Using the data

You are going to draw evidence from your data to back up any statements and claims you may make. Consider how often you hear substantial claims made without a shred of evidence:

- 'My clients are much happier with this product.'
- 'Things have improved since the new computer system was put in.'
- 'The situation is better under the present government.'

Where is the evidence? Whose opinion is being expressed here? Who judges the truth of these statements?

These issues are becoming increasingly important in the literatures of qualitative research, case study, action research, life history and other new paradigm research methodologies. Researchers have been known to make substantial claims for their research without producing validated evidence. Make sure you do not fall into the same trap. When your reader comes across such statements as 'My patients said they were happier with the service', or 'Nurses learned the material more effectively through interaction with the video pack than from other resource material', they will expect to see or hear evidence from the patients and nurses themselves, and not just take your word for it. As a general rule, you should not speak on behalf of your research participants; otherwise you are potentially distorting the data and its analysis. You should find every opportunity for creating ways for them to speak for themselves.

You can of course produce various forms of evidence to back up your claims. It may be in quantitative form, or in documentary or other appropriate form. You may want to produce still photos to underscore your interpretation of what is happening. You may refer to audio- or video-taped evidence that corroborates what you are saying. You could cross-reference your fieldnotes and submit those as evidence. Whatever form your evidence takes, it must be there. Advice about techniques for dealing with the data appears in Chapter 8. Advice about turning data into evidence appears in Chapter 9.

How to involve other people in the monitoring process

At the beginning of this chapter we said that monitoring the action is more complicated than simply collecting data about how you perform an aspect of your work. We suggested that it involved three distinct operations:

1   Collecting data about the action so that it provides the clearest possible description of what has happened.
2   Interpreting the data you have collected so that you can develop a tentative explanation of what has happened.
3   Evaluating what you have done so that you can plan further action.

Other people can help you make a disciplined and critical study of your practices in relation to each of these operations. Co-operation and colla-boration are integral to action research due to its nature as an educational practice. The following two ideas, drawn from Pam Lomax's six principles of action research (Lomax, 1994a), are central:

- that action research is participatory and others are involved as co-researchers rather than informants, so that critical communities of people are formed;
- that action research is about sharing ideas, interpretations and conclu-sions with an 'educated' audience, who are able and willing to judge the authenticity and relevance of the work to a particular professional context.

In line with these principles, you need to develop relationships with others in which you:

- ask them to give critical feedback about your action;
- encourage them to share the educational experience of being an action researcher;
- persuade them to become co-researchers;
- are prepared to relinquish your ownership of the action if they are ready to take it over.

You will be most successful here if:

- you are open and avoid manipulating others;
- you are prepared to take risks and sometimes expose others to risk;
- you make your research transparent;
- you are clear about the ethical principles than govern your collaboration.

Who do you involve?

Start small and establish a working relationship with one or two work colleagues who are willing to provide critical but supportive friendship. These colleagues become critical friends, or critical colleagues. We authors use the term differently from some other writers (e.g. Bayne-Jardine and Holly, 1994) who see a critical friend as an outsider process consultant. In our view, a critical friend is expected to act as a confidant/e or mentor and talk through the research at regular intervals, preferably from an insider perspective. Because critical friends are assumed to know the research context well, they can help you deal with the micro-politics of work. Sometimes they are chosen because their position in their organisation empowers researchers and adds support to influencing change. This is a perfectly acceptable situation, because researchers are often expected to negotiate the focus of their research with senior colleagues so that the work has organisational as well as personal benefit. The critical friend, regardless of status or role, is expected to help you achieve a critical perspective – what some philosophers call 'rendering the familiar strange' – even though this may challenge the normal assumptions underlying your work. Critique can be hard to achieve, especially when you and your critical friend share the same values and assumptions, but it is essential to maintain the integrity of what you are doing.

What part do they play in validating your research?

The idea of validation appeared earlier and will be dealt with in more detail in Chapter 9. When action research is carried out in an institution, it is common procedure to ask critical friends to join validation groups that have been set up to validate a colleague's action research. They can help in the following ways:

- as witnesses, confirming and verifying that the research had taken place in the way in which it was described;
- as helping the researcher give a good account of their research;
- as offering an evaluation ('critical partnerships');
- as giving moral support for the researcher in terms of encouragement, positive feedback and sympathetic support.

(Lomax *et al.*, 1996)

Who can act as a critical friend?

You decide who will act as your critical friend/s. Decide on one or two special people drawn from your wider circle of personal and professional contacts. Make sure they will be supportive, but not so supportive that they do not provide critique. They may be drawn from anyone in your circle: managers, colleagues, students, family. They must be available to you when needed, so you need to negotiate with them how often you will meet, what you expect of them, and what they can expect from you.

Sometimes the critical friendship is seen as one of potential collusion. Collusion is obviously unfortunate, because some people may think your research was legitimated because you are a nice person, rather than because it is methodologically rigorous and has its own integrity. Your research should be judged on its own merits, so it is important to negotiate with your critical friends how you will assess the research, and then make this public to anyone who wants to know. The critical friendship relationship should be educational for you and your friends. It is important to establish a trusting relationship in which you can establish the grounds for giving and receiving critique.

Now that you have a good idea about the main ideas underpinning monitoring, and you have given thought to how to involve others in your research, you can begin to think about how you will deal with your data. Dealing with the data is the focus of Chapter 8.

Chapter 8

Techniques for dealing with the data

This chapter provides a guide to techniques for building an archive of data that may be used as evidence within action research case studies. Each section deals with a specific technique. The chapter has sections on:

- Using a research diary
- Observation methods
- Questionnaires
- Interviews
- Photography, audio- and videotape-recordings and interactive media

Using a research diary

People keep diaries for a variety of reasons: to record their thoughts and feelings about the daily events of life, to remind them of future appointments, and to give them a record of these events when they are past. Research diaries are no different from ordinary diaries, other than that they focus on issues to do with the research. So you need to consider in advance how you are going to use what you write, and this will influence how you organise your diary.

Consider the following ideas about how a research diary may be used:

- It may be used to make a **time-line**. Keeping a clear time-line is important. Aim to log everything with a date and time, make a note about the context where appropriate, and anything else you feel could be significant.

- It may be used to illustrate **general points**. Particularly important are 'thick' descriptions that show the complexities of a situation rather than 'thin' descriptions that present the situation as unproblematic.
- It may be used as **raw data** that is subjected to analysis. This means that the diary itself will go into your data archive and provide a potentially rich source of evidence.
- It may be used to **chart the progress** of your action research including successful or unsuccessful action and the personal learning that emerges from your reflection on this.

Some writers differentiate between the terms 'log', 'journal' and 'diary', suggesting that each should be a record of different types of data. Others suggest that different kinds of journal writing should be used for different kinds of thinking. These distinctions are not always necessary and they can be confusing. It is up to you to decide what you want to call your diary and how you want to use it, but you must be clear about its purpose and the types of entry you intend to make in it.

You should maintain your diary throughout your research project. In the early stages of the research many people feel unsure about report writing, and diary writing is often easier. Whatever you write, it will probably provide you with some documentation to return to and reflect on. Try to establish good habits from the start; if you don't, you could later seriously regret not keeping systematic entries.

Your diary may serve one or several of the following purposes:

- A regularly kept and systematic record of factual information about events, dates and people. You may organise it under headings such as When? Where? What? Who? Which? How? Why? The data you record should help you construct a chronological time-line, or recon-struct events as a description of what has happened.
- An *aide-mémoire* to record short notes and ideas about your research for later reflection.
- A detailed portrait of particular events and situations which will provide richly descriptive data to be used later in written accounts.
- A record of anecdotes and passing observations, informed conversations and subjective impressions that are largely unplanned. In this sort of diary it would be important to log exact words in order to quote them in later accounts.
- An introspective and self-evaluative account in which you record your personal experiences, thoughts and feelings with a view to trying to understand your own action. This may provide convincing evidence of the processes of your own learning and indicate connections between actions and outcomes.

- A comforting companion, particularly in times of stress when you need to jettison unwanted anxieties, until you feel better able to face up to them.
- A reflective account that enables you to understand an experience better by reflecting on it privately. This kind of reflective work can be therapeutic, as well as creatively helping you find new ways of making sense of things.
- An analytical process to help you examine your data on an ongoing basis. You would be able to keep records in a variety of forms, and track for yourself how these show how your thinking changed over time.
- A place in which criteria emerge to enable you to judge progress.
- A way of distancing yourself from your action in order to interrogate it. You could use your diary entries as texts that could be subject to different sorts of textual analysis. For example, if you were concerned about possible gender bias in your work you could look at the sorts of metaphor you use to describe events and people, or at the entries you have made concerning people of different genders.

Collaborative diary keeping and diaries kept by other people

Collaborative diary keeping

If you are engaged in a collaborative project with one or more other people, you may decide to triangulate your diary entries. Triangulation is where you use data about an event from more than one source, for example:

- You and your partner may be working together but keeping separate diaries in order to check out your different interpretations of events.
- You and your partner may be working in separate contexts on a shared concern and using your diary entries to compare your different situations and responses.

Some researchers use an interactive diary in which they write comments in response to each other's reflections.

Diaries kept by other participants

You may keep a diary yourself and ask other participants to keep similar diaries which you could use to check out your own interpretations. You would have to ask their permission to use their diaries as your data. Although in such cases you would be on the outside of the participant's action, you would be able to make a judgement about your own educative influence in the life of your participant. If you are an outsider to the action, you would need to take special care to reflect on the nature of your relationship with the participant in order to render your use of their responses as transparent and open as possible, as well as making sure that they agreed with your use of the data.

This emphasises the need for good ethical conduct throughout. If you have permission to use other people's diaries, you must check that you have used their work in a way that is acceptable to them. This means submitting your reports to the people concerned in order to obtain their approval before you go to print. You also need to establish if anonymity should be maintained, or if the participant wishes to be acknowledged and thanked.

Maintaining a research diary

Diary writing may not come naturally to you, so you have to be disciplined. The effort can be worthwhile. Make sure you write regularly and that you set aside time for this as an integral part of your research process. Build it in as part of your systematic reflection on progress. You do not need to write every day, but aim to develop a schedule, and stick to it. Make a contract with yourself to do this. Remember, you will also need time out to reflect upon what you have written and periodic time to review and build on insights.

Before you begin, or soon after, decide the following:

- Will you need to keep more than one diary to cope with the different purposes to which you will put it?
- Should you divide your diary into sections for different purposes? Some people divide the page into half, labelling one half 'What I did' and the other half 'What I learned'. You could also have a third section labelled 'What I learned through my learning'. It is up to you to decide; it's your diary for your use.
- Do you need to develop a system of cross-referencing between parts of your single diary or between diaries kept for different purposes?
- Should you keep your diary in a loose-leaf folder with sections that may be used for specific material, rather like a personal organiser?
- Could your diary take a completely different form such as a card index system in which items are sorted, or a 'talking diary', using a tape-recorder in which brief notes may be made for later digestion or expansion?
- How will you design each page? Will you leave space for additional notes made at a later date?
- Will you keep some parts of your diary for private reflections and other parts for writing that you could make public?

- Will you use your diary to record data collected by other research methods such as observations or interviews?

Finally . . .

- Keep a small notebook for quick notes that can be transferred to your main diary later.
- Periodically review and summarise your diary. This is important for identifying connections and patterns in your data.
- Get into the habit of reading some of your diary entries to a critical friend and inviting discussion.

Observation methods

In a sense, all research begins with observation. You systematically watch what is happening and record your observations. In action research you aim to watch yourself, and you also watch other people to check how you are influencing them in an educational way. Because you are at the centre of the action it is not always possible to observe yourself, so you need to find ways of doing this, such as using video, or asking other people to observe you. For example, Rod Linter (1989) made video-recordings of his lessons and then used the Flanders Interaction Analysis Chart (FIAC) to analyse classroom interaction. He did this as part of an action research design in which he wanted to know if a modification of his teaching had been successful in increasing students' participation in his lessons. His research is interesting because he invited a colleague to help him apply the FIAC instrument to the videoed lesson in order to strengthen his confidence in the analysis. The results of the initial analysis enabled him to reflect on what was happening in the classroom and to take action to modify it. His first analysis revealed:

> a high level of direction and limited opportunity for pupils to express their ideas . . . equally alarming was the revelation that out of a class of 24 students, twelve remained silent, nine of them girls.
>
> (Linter, 1989: 91)

If you are a member of a team, your colleagues will probably be willing to observe you or allow you to observe them. Excellent examples of professionals who systematically carried out reciprocal observations and used their negotiated findings for their individual research projects are in Delong (2002). Jackie Delong tells of how she arranged for school principals to observe one another as well as observe herself as superintendent.

Devising your own observation schedule may suit your purposes better than an off-the-peg version such as the FIAC. If you decide to design your own you need to consider the following:

- What is the purpose of the observation? What do you want to find out?
- Which particular pieces of the action are you observing? Is it all equally important?
- How will you use the data?
- Have you considered ethical issues throughout?

Here are some well-tried strategies for charting observation data.

Head counting

This is straightforward. You simply count the number of times a particular event happened; for example, how many times a person speaks. It is well-nigh impossible to watch all the action at the same time in a particular situation, so aim to be selective and break it down into time blocks over a designated period of time. For example, Margaret Follows (1989) broke down her observations into time blocks that occurred daily for a specified period each morning and afternoon. During these times she observed whether the children who were engaged in each of eight activities came from one class, two classes or three classes. After five weeks she was able to produce the following chart (Table 8.1).

Table 8.1 The class unit composition of pupils engaged in observed activities each week

	Week 1	Week 2	Week 3	Week 4	Week 5
From one class	77%	31%	51%	32%	37%
From two classes	20%	64%	20%	46%	25%
From three classes	3%	4%	20%	22%	37%
Number of activities	35	45	35	41	51

Interaction charting

The idea of interaction charting is to draw a graphic that communicates dynamically what is going on. For example, Figure 8.1 shows how you could chart interactions among people. The small cross-lines indicate the number of times different people interact. The arrows show who speaks to whom.

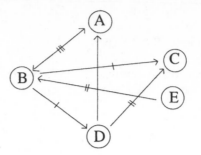

Figure 8.1 Sociometric analysis

Procedural analysis

This kind of exercise requires you to draw up an agenda, or time plan of a specific event, and then to plot the actions and interactions within the frame. For example, McTaggart (1990) wanted to find out who spoke most in a staff meeting. He used a frame in which he listed the names of the people in the meeting along one axis and the amount of time they spoke along another. From this he was able to identify the number of contributions that individuals made in the meeting and the length of time for which they spoke. Because he participated in the meeting himself, he tape-recorded the meeting and used the tape to check his findings. Table 8.2 records the results of his observations.

Table 8.2 Participation analysis. Staff meeting 1 March 1989

Participant	No. of contributions	Length of time (m.s.)	Total talk time (%)
Mr M	42	18.41	49.7
Head	36	9.29	25.2
Mrs S	14	2.25	6.4
Mr B	21	3.35	9.5
Mrs M	13	1.19	3.5
Mr A	6	1.10	3.5
Mrs B	6	0.13	0.5
Mrs A	1	0.02	0
Mrs R	6	0.23	1.0
Miss C	5	0.17	0.7
Mrs C	0	0.00	0
Total	150	36.14	100

Source: McTaggart, 1990: 75

Interaction-process analysis

This kind of charting analysis may be used in a variety of ways. For example, the Flanders Interaction Analysis Chart used by Linter (page 118) operates by way of a grid, and is used to capture the number and type of interpersonal interaction. This technique may be used to capture sophisticated interactions, but is demanding in concentration. You need to be familiar with the categories of behaviour you have devised as indicators of the action that you are watching. For example, Table 8.3 shows the kind of schedule you could use if you wanted to see the types of interaction that take place in a conversation.

Table 8.3 Record sheet to show conversation categories

Categories of behaviour	One-minute intervals						
Smiles							
Touches							
Nods							
Initiates conversation							
Listens							
Is empathic							

Observation data of the kind described in this section may be useful for tracking changes in a variety of situations over time; for example, in the relationships between yourself and a group of people, or among the people themselves. You could use the same observation schedule at regular intervals for six weeks. Observation schedules can be greatly enhanced when they are used in conjunction with audio and video records, or where they are used co-operatively by a group.

Questionnaires

First-time researchers often rush into producing questionnaires without sufficiently considering what is involved. This can be dangerous. Issuing a questionnaire is a political act because questionnaires are not neutral. They can influence their respondents and alert them to ideas they had not thought about before. For example, if you send a questionnaire to parents asking if their children are being bullied at school, they may get the idea that bullying is occurring.

The responses from questionnaires can often be misleading. Moira Cluskey points out that respondents can be unreliable. 'If I ask my students today if they enjoy school I may get a 60% answer in the affirmative. If I ask the same question tomorrow the result may have dropped to 50%. This reduction may be caused by a variety of factors' (Cluskey, 1996: 4).

In this section you will find some common-sense ideas about questionnaire construction and use. The basic advice is: do not use a questionnaire unless you have a good reason for doing so.

There are two reasons for using a questionnaire within an action research design:

- to find out information that cannot be ascertained otherwise;
- to evaluate the effect of an intervention when it is inappropriate to get feedback in another way.

You may also wish to use a questionnaire in order to introduce a particular idea to a chosen audience. The example about bullying suggests that questionnaires may be used to pave the way for new ideas.

Some preliminary points:

- Establish why you want the information. Is it essential to your project?
- If you already know the answers do not use a questionnaire.
- Never ask questions if you can get the information elsewhere. If people have to answer too many questions, they will probably not return the questionnaire.
- If it is to be a postal survey, can you afford it? Remember you will probably have to send out reminders.
- If you want to ask a representative sample of people, you need to read about sampling procedures in a specialised book on the subject.
- Will you need to gain access to the people whom you wish to question? Have you the necessary permission?
- If you are intending to send a questionnaire to colleagues at work, are you sure that this is the best way of getting your answers?

Constructing questionnaires

Collingwood (1939) said that there are no 'correct' answers. There are only 'right' answers that will keep the dialogue open. The same idea applies to questionnaires. There are no 'correct' questions or answers, but there are appropriate questions and answers that can move things forward. Always ask, 'Is this question appropriate? Is it going to give me the kind of feedback that will help me move my thinking forward?'

Different kinds of questions exist, including closed and open questions, and these serve different purposes.

Closed questions have a restricted format, such as ticking a particular box which contains a pre-specified answer. The advantage of closed questions is that they require less space for answers, and the answers are easier to tally. Their limitations are that you will not get back any answers that fall outside the range you have specified.

Open questions allow the respondent to express a broader range of ideas. An open question is of the kind, 'What do you think about . . .?' Open questions require more space for answers. You will also find these open questions more time-consuming to analyse, because they can be diverse and rich in ideas. However, even an open question closes off possibilities because it sets boundaries for possible answers.

Questionnaire construction is a technical business. If you want to do it well you should first read a good text on questionnaire construction. Then you should try it out on a few friends to make sure your questions make sense. Pilot it again on a different audience, one that is familiar with the kind of situation you are exploring. Always show it to your tutor (if you have one) and to your critical friends. Aim to pilot the questionnaire several times. Remember: questionnaires can ruin the research context for you if they are inappropriate.

If you decide to use a questionnaire, here is some advice on procedure.

Guidelines for administering a questionnaire

- Decide what information you need to find out. Construct your questionnaire or use one that has already been piloted. Put the instructions for completing the questionnaire at the top of the paper.
- Be polite, and ask your participants to help. At the end of the questionnaire, thank your participants. Make a statement to say that you will inform them of the results if they wish.
- Have a clear policy for dealing with confidentiality and share this with your respondents.
- Clearly write or type your questionnaire. Leave enough space for the respondent to write their answers easily. Clearly number or otherwise annotate your items. Use good-quality paper. Pay attention to detail in content and appearance.
- If you photocopy the questionnaire, make sure that the copies are clear and legible.
- Pilot the questionnaire. Try it out on a few people and invite their critique. Analyse the responses to see if it is giving you the kind of data you want.
- Run the questionnaire. Give your respondents a fixed time in which to return it. Write on the questionnaire itself when you would like it

returned. If you want people to send it back to you, provide postage and envelopes.

Interviews

Interviews are used in a variety of research contexts and are used frequently within an action research design. Because action research always aims to be educational, interviews are likely to be informal discussions rather than formal interviews. Sometimes formal interviews are appropriate, in order to establish some information or to evaluate an outcome, much in the same way as described for questionnaires. More often they aim to develop conversations that lead to enhanced insights for all participants.

Interviews have distinct advantages over questionnaires because they provide richer data as a result of being able to probe further.

Interviews range from fully structured to open, with variations between these extremes.

A fully structured interview is really the face-to-face delivery of a questionnaire. The interviewer must ask the questions exactly as they appear on the interview schedule. The aim is to provide exactly the same questions, in the same order and style of delivery, to all interviewees.

An open interview has a starting point and an objective, but no set agenda of questions. The interviewer should be free to follow where the interviewee leads as long as it is within the general framework.

Choosing between open and closed interviews would depend on their purpose. If the interview is part of a formal evaluation, it would probably be more structured than if it were to establish what sort of situation existed prior to commencing the research.

Guidelines for conducting interviews

- Aim to document the interview unobtrusively. You can use some of the procedures for documenting data described in Chapter 7 if they are appropriate, such as the use of notebooks, audiotape- and videotape-recording. Always let the person you are interviewing know that you are doing this.
- Be clear about the ethics of interviewing. These are similar to those for all kinds of research.
- Tell your inteviewees what the interview is about, or tell them that you are unable to do so.
- Do not mislead or deceive people in order to persuade them to share information.
- Be prepared to maintain complete confidentiality if this is requested. You must honour your commitment.

- Develop good listening skills. Active listening includes controlling your body language, so that the person whom you are interviewing knows that you are interested and value what they say.
- Learn to give verbal and visual cues to encourage your interviewee to talk freely.
- Learn to sense when it is appropriate to feed back what the interviewee is saying, in order to help them maintain their flow. For example, you may say, 'Now, as I understand it, you are saying that . . .'
- Show that you empathise with your interviewee's position so that they feel confident to expand on what they are saying.
- Learn to accept silences, and be silent yourself. Silences are important spaces in which people gather their thoughts or harness their courage.
- Practise using possible 'framing questions' that help keep the conversation going. For example:

  - *Clarifying questions* to elucidate something the speaker has said: 'Can I check that, please?'
  - *Probing questions* to explore an issue that the speaker has raised: 'Can we discuss that a little further?'
  - *Context-specific questions* that check (1) that the interviewee is at ease with the question: 'Is it all right for us to talk about this?', or (2) that the interviewee understands the question: 'Can I ask you to put that question in your own words?', or (3) that the interviewee is comfortable with your own performance: 'Have I said that correctly?'

Photography, audio- and videotape-recordings and interactive media

Recent developments in the use of interactive media have given massive opportunities for representing and authenticating research in new ways. It is possible today to show the 'live' action of the research process using multiple forms of representation at the same time: videotape-recordings, still photographs, live conversations, links through an oral or written text. Each day brings new possibilities through developing technologies.

It is important to ensure that you have full permission from all participants before you gather data using audio-visual forms of representation. This permission may have to be in writing, depending on your context. Some authorities have recently banned unauthorised audio-visual records for fear that the records may be used for illegal purposes. Always check with your manager or principal beforehand.

For the sake of analysis, we shall look separately at the features of different technologies, but bear in mind that it is possible to combine all of them in interactive presentations, and to interact with the data in a manner that enables you to make sense of the data in ways previously unavailable.

Photography

The main use of photography in action research is to document action, but it may also be used as part of monitoring and evaluation strategies. Have a look at the work of Jon Prosser (1998) and Michael Schratz (2000) for pioneering ideas about how photography may be used. Here are some ideas for you to consider.

- Photographs can show changes over time. For example, Mary McTiernan (1997) showed how, over time, the geographical rearrangement of the tables in her adult education classroom facilitated greater participation and a diffusion of power from herself to participants.
- Photographs can show the quality of people's engagement in an activity. Hannon (1996) photographed hospitalised children to show their engagement with materials in the science boxes she had designed for them.
- Photographs may be used for stimulated recall. People can talk about their experience using photographs. This technique may also be used in an interviewing situation to prompt the memory.
- Photographs can be used as evidence that an event has taken place. Remember to date the photograph.
- Photographs can be used within self-study as the focus for deconstructing personal memories.
- Different photographs of the same event from different perspectives can be used to stimulate discussion about what people see rather than what they believe they are expected to see.

Audiotape-recording

Tape-recorders are an invaluable piece of equipment for action researchers. Try to obtain your own small tape-recorder and carry it around with you. You can record data in all the ways suggested for photographs. A tape-recorder has the added advantage that it can be used as a talking diary or as a way of catching informal conversations and discussions about your research. As noted above, it may be used to capture conversations when you are observing a meeting so that you can edit or construct observation charts later. We authors encourage our groups to tape-record their evaluation conversations about their own progress. We then transcribe the tapes and the transcripts go up on the group's web space for further use by group members. (*Note:* we all sign letters of permission for one another to ensure confidentiality.)

This brings us to the business of transcribing. Using audiotape-recording means you will probably have to make a transcript later. This is a lengthy procedure, and should be undertaken only if you are sure that this is the best way of dealing with the data. A transcript of a conversation gives the full flavour of the meanings, but usually you will require only excerpts or parts of the whole. One way of dealing with this is to use the tape counter and to write at intervals and in summarised form what the tape contains. Then transcribe only those parts of the tape you wish to quote. Use these quotations in the main body of your report. Put the transcripts into the appendices or into the archive, whichever is appropriate. Use your judgement. Put the tape itself into the archive.

The data on the tape is not there only to add to the content of your report. You will want to listen to your tapes on more than one occasion in order to reflect on and evaluate the action that has been captured. You may even want to play them to critical friends. These are very important times in the monitoring process, and there is nothing as versatile or rigorously documented as taped materials.

Videotape-recording

The development of digital technologies such as camcorders and video-recorders has made videotape-recording accessible to all in recent years. Video is as near to reality as it is possible to get. The use of interactive media enables the recorded reality to be stored for later retrieval, or edited or evaluated on the spot.

Video captures the non-verbal, as well as the verbal, messages that are being sent. This is important for self-studies that make claims about a person's educative influence in another's life. It is often more effective to show how one person reacted to another through a visual recording than only through verbal descriptions. Video shows the embodied meanings people bring to their work, and helps us move beyond word pictures of reality to real visual pictures of reality.

Video-recordings may be used in most of the ways listed for photographs and audiotape, but they are better for capturing changes in behaviour in both individuals and groups. They have the added advantage that you can set the camera and video your own practice. By looking at the videotapes of yourself in company with others, you can check whether or not you are doing what you believe you should be doing, or whether you are seeing yourself as a living contradiction, and why this may be happening. If you look at the videotapes with your critical friend, you may find good ideas to help you decide what to do in order to improve things. Chapter 12 continues the discussion about video and its uses in action research.

Now that you have read this chapter, you should have a good idea of the range of techniques you can use to collect your data. Remember, in action research, you should use these techniques within a philosophy of monitoring outlined in Chapter 7, and regard them as resources you can use to improve your own practice.

Part V

Making claims to knowledge and validating them

When you say you have learned something, you are making a claim that you now know something that was not known before. This is your original claim to knowledge. If the knowledge is to be taken seriously as knowledge, and not opinion or conjecture, it has to be validated; that is, agreed by someone else to be justifiably believable. Doing this can be problematic, because not all participants may agree on what counts as valid knowledge, and which criteria and standards of judgement should be used in coming to this decision.

Part V deals with these issues. Chapter 9 is about making claims and validating them. Chapter 10 is about which criteria and standards of judgement are used, and some of the frequent dilemmas posed in legitimation processes.

Chapter 9

Making claims to knowledge and validating them

This chapter contains the following sections:

- What does making claims to knowledge mean?
- What does validating mean, what is validated, and who does the validating?
- When we speak about reaching agreement, what forms of agreement exist, and what is needed for the claim to knowledge to be legitimated?

You should read this chapter in conjunction with Chapter 10, because issues of claims to knowledge, validity claims, evidence, criteria, standards of judgement and legitimation processes are all part of the same field. The two chapters are organised to present the ideas analytically. In real life, the issues always go together.

What does making claims to knowledge mean?

In Chapter 1 we said that all research has the aim of advancing knowledge. In doing your research, you are aiming to create new knowledge. In presenting your research to others, you are saying that you have done this. In asking them to validate your new knowledge, you are asking them also to validate your assumptions about the knowledge-generating process; that is, how you believe you have come to know. These assumptions include the following.

The generation of new meanings

The social intent of your research was to improve your particular situation. Improvement would probably have occurred because you, working with other people, improved your understanding of what you were doing. You were working collaboratively, so you were clarifying for one another what this meant for you and your work. You were negotiating and constructing your own meanings out of your shared practices. In this way you were advancing your individual and collective knowing.

Making tacit knowledge explicit

People have a deep reservoir of tacit knowledge (or personal or intuitive knowledge). This knowledge is usually hidden, even to the person who has this knowledge, and often cannot be articulated. It is manifested in different ways, for example, knowing that you are cold and putting on another jumper, or knowing what someone is going to say before they say it. Many researchers draw on the idea of tacit knowledge as the basis of good practice (see e.g. Nonaka and Takeuchi, 1995; Sternberg and Horvath, 1999). They explain how organisations may be improved by encouraging people first to share their tacit knowledge about their work, and then to go through processes of making this knowledge more and more explicit: first to share their values, and then to find ways in which they can live out these values.

You are claiming that you have done this in your research. You articulated your values, and you probably also identified a situation in which these values were being denied in some way. You decided to take action to improve the situation, first by improving your understanding of how you were positioned in that situation. You began to make your tacit knowledge explicit. You and others worked collaboratively to raise your collective tacit knowledge about your shared values to a conscious level. You offered reasons for your actions. You are able to show how you deliberately tried to exercise your educative influence, so that other people became more reflective and aware of their positioning in social situations, in order also to take action to improve those situations by influencing others. In this way you are able to demonstrate your accountability, how your actions are underpinned by a moral commitment, and how you are aiming to help people develop the same kind of moral awareness. You are aiming to transform practice into praxis at an individual and collective level.

Contributing to the wider body of knowledge

You are claiming that you have generated new knowledge out of the processes of shared story-telling, and you are explaining that story-telling is a form of research that is validated in terms of its own criteria. These criteria are different from traditional ones.

The hallmarks of the old scholarships of traditional research are replicability and generalisability. Research is held to be good quality if people can do the same thing with the same results, and if the method and its findings can be generalised to all similar situations.

These criteria are inappropriate for the new scholarships of action research. It is neither possible nor desirable to aim for replication or generalisation, since the aim is to understand rather than predict, to liberate rather than control. People do research on themselves, not on others; they do research with others in order to understand and improve their social practices. People offer stories of their own improved understanding as outcomes. They share those stories, not competitively but collaboratively. This shared learning can lead to the construction of collective knowledge.

Traditional forms of scholarship believe that a self-contained body of knowledge exists in books and artefacts. If people go away and leave the books behind, the knowledge continues to exist in the books. New forms of scholarship believe that knowledge is always being created, and exists in people and the stories they tell. These stories may appear in book form, but the books are books that tell experience, not books that tell only facts. People tell their stories to other people, and those other people restory the originals into their own stories (Connelly and Clandinin, 1990). The accumulation of individual stories constitutes a culture of collective learning. The stories, and the knowledge they represent, are always in transformation; what is known today can transform into a new form tomorrow.

These shared stories do not represent group-think but a community of independent thinkers, each willing to submit their claim to knowledge to the critique of others, to ensure that their claim is robust and legitimate. Sometimes researchers working in traditional ways criticise action researchers for not maintaining standards of rigorous scholarship. On the contrary, action research represents a new form of scholarship that both respects and sometimes incorporates traditional standards, and also creates new standards to test new forms of practices that focus on demonstrating originality of mind and critical engagement. It demands intellectual independence and also honesty and responsibility. Validation methods involve ensuring that claims to knowledge are tested and approved by the most rigorous standards.

Formative and summative evaluation

You are claiming that you can show the processes of ongoing evaluation throughout your project, in terms of how your consideration of your current learning has led to new improved learning.

Your research question was, 'How do I improve . . . ?' Your research project shows the processes you went through to improve. These processes
possibly involved working your way through several cycles. Each cycle
comprised periods of action, followed by periods of reflection (perhaps
these happened almost simultaneously), followed by new actions that
were informed by the insights that emerged from your reflections. Your
research processes probably took the form of identification of an issue,
imagination of a solution, implementation of the solution, gathering of
evidence, evaluation of the solution and modification of practice.
Although you might present these stages as straightforward sequences
of events, you explain that the realities were not so neat, and the research
process probably involved a lot of backtracking and criss-crossing.

You might present your project as constituting only one cycle of action
and reflection, or it could constitute several cycles. Turning your project
into several cycles can make it easier to handle, because one cycle contains
the seeds of the next within itself. Any provisional answers you come to in
one cycle will contain a new question for the next. For example, Geoff
Mead's (2001) Ph.D. thesis shows how questions can develop during the
course of the enquiry. The question 'How can I improve my practice as a
learning support teacher?' that Thérèse Ó Riordan-Burke (1997) asked
for her Master's dissertation work transformed into a new question: 'How
do I exercise my educative influence in creating conditions for critical
learning?', for her doctoral study.

You explain how you have evaluated each cycle, to show what you
learned, what you still needed to do at this stage, and how this phase
was already transforming into a new phase. In presenting each cycle you
would have made intermediate claims in the form of progress reports,
and you would have presented evidence in support of your claims. These
reports were your formative (ongoing) evaluation, to check whether you
were on track in relation to your original research question. At the end
of each cycle, you would have offered a summative (concluding) evaluation statement, to show that you had addressed your research question,
at least in part. If your project took the form of several cycles, you would
have aimed to produce ongoing progress reports (formative evaluation
statements) at strategic times during the research. Your summative
evaluation of each cycle then became the starting point of the next. You
explain that, although you have broken the process down into separate
parts to explain it in an analytical way, the whole thing was seamless
and transformational. You also explain that, while the process of doing
the research might appear chaotic, there was in fact a deep underlying
order to the work, and this order began to emerge during the synthesising
process of making the claim to knowledge available for public scrutiny,
usually through writing up but also via other forms of representation.

Making validity claims

In presenting your work you are making all these validity claims about your new knowledge and about the processes that have led to this new knowledge. They are validity claims because you are making claims to validity with supporting evidence. You explain that your new knowledge has emerged through the processes. The knowledge has not been 'given'; it has been created. You explain how your knowledge generation processes are transformations of embodied knowledge into explicit knowledge, which you are now able to stand over and claim as your original contribution to the wider literature. You are now asking for your validity claims to be legitimated by the external world of researchers.

What does validating mean, what is validated, and who does the validating?

There is an important distinction between validation and legitimation. This is not always clear in the literature. Validating refers to the process of testing the truthfulness of a knowledge claim by making it public for critical scrutiny in relation to appropriate standards of judgement. Legitimation refers to the power relations that determine what counts as truth in a particular context. Remember what happened to Galileo when he presented his claim to know that the earth orbited the sun. He had good evidence for believing this, and had tested the validity of his claim in relation to the evidence. Because the Church could exercise power in deciding what was legitimate knowledge and had decreed that the sun orbited the earth, Galileo was shown instruments of torture as if they were to be used, and he recanted what he knew to be valid. In this case the processes of legitimation had rejected what was valid because it conflicted with the received wisdom of the day that was upheld by a set of power relations.

In this chapter we deal with issues of validation. In Chapter 10 we focus more on issues of legitimation.

It is straightforward enough to make a claim and to produce evidence, but, unless other people agree with you, your research will not be regarded as credible. Your claim could be construed as your own opinion. Remember: data is not evidence. When you say you have done something (your claim) you need to have available as evidence those pieces of data that you understand as in relation to your criteria and that show your criteria in action (see Chapter 10 for issues about criteria). Other people consider your claim, in relation to your evidence, and they then agree that you are justified in making your claim or they recommend that you think again or make adjustments, either to your practice or to your report (for example, include more evidence, or evidence of a different nature).

Forms of validation

There are different forms of validation.

Self-validation

As a responsible practitioner, can you show to your own satisfaction that you have done the things you set out to do? Can you show that you have carried out a systematic enquiry to help you live in the direction of your values more effectively than before? Can you offer an account of your own professional learning, and show that your influence has been educative for the people you are with?

Peer validation

Can you convince a group of peers that your claim to knowledge should be taken seriously? Will they agree that you are demonstrating responsible practice? Do you offer clear criteria for the assessment of your work, and produce unambiguous evidence in relation to those criteria?

Up-liner validation

Can you show to managers and those in authority that you have intervened in your practice to improve it, and that your way of working could be adopted, for example, in institutional development plans?

Client validation

Will the people whom you are supporting agree that you have acted in their interests, and that the quality of life is better because of your intervention?

Academic validation

Will the academic community agree that you have contributed to a recognised body of knowledge? If you are on an award-bearing course you will have to submit your work for established forms of examination. Significant progress has been made in how dissertations and theses are judged, and many examiners understand what new scholarship enquiries involve and how they should be judged.

The general public

Your final validation group will be the wider community of readers in organisational or general contexts. Going public is the subject of Chapter 12, which deals with issues of getting published and targeting particular publication outlets. It may take time for your work to be widely accepted. Ideas about what is considered good scholarship can take time to mature. Fortunately, work in previous years has established solid precedents for practitioner enquiry as a legitimate form of research, and many case studies are available to offer exemplars of what it looks like and how it should be judged. However, political trends still dominate in education research and influence what is to be seen as legitimate. It can even come to the level of who is in fashion and who has a following of admirers. The test of ideas, however, is not in the person but in the durability of the ideas, and how they may be shown to work for human betterment. Individuals may be forgotten. Good ideas last in the lives of other people.

The validation group

Validating in action research contexts involves submitting your research to the judgement of a group of relevant others; that is, inviting their legitimation. This group could be made up of members of any of the groups listed above and may vary in size and formality.

A validating group needs to comprise individuals who are sympathetic to the research, but who are able and prepared to give critical feedback. There can be a real dilemma here in protecting the emergent thinking of the researcher while also giving the critique that will move forward the researcher's thinking (Lomax, 1994a). There is no point in inviting people who are hostile or indifferent to your research to be in your validation group. You do, however, need to establish a group that is prepared to be critical, to avoid possible challenges of collusion. Your work needs to stand on its own merit, and therefore you need to include people in your group who would view the work with a cautious and critical eye.

It is helpful, though not always possible, to identify the people whom you wish to be in your validating group from the start of your project, and invite them to take part. Make sure that the size of the group is conducive to the work that needs to be done. The group should not number more than ten, and would usually comprise four or five members. Explain their responsibilities (page 00), and that they are making a commitment for the duration. Ideally you should have much the same group throughout, so that they will be able to comment on your progress by comparing and contrasting events such as critical incidents. They will also be able to judge the development of your own professional learning. Give your group a list of dates when you would like them to be available to work on your reports with you: once every two months, perhaps. The intervals depend on your circumstances and the willingness and availability of your group. It is much easier for people to meet together if they are work-ing in the same organisation. If people have to travel, organising meetings is more difficult and calls for careful forward planning.

The final validation meeting would aim to look at the overall report (summative evaluation), together with all the evidence, when the group would agree (or not) that the claim to knowledge is a valid claim, that is, the research is credible, so that this knowledge may be put into the public domain and acted on by others.

Sometimes validation procedures are part of formal programmes, such as the Master's and Doctoral programmes where we authors work. In those contexts action researchers are given specific guidance about the constitution of the validation group, the materials to be presented and the form the criteria should take. At the end of this chapter there is an example of a briefing sheet which applies to these formal meetings.

At other times, how you conduct the validating sessions is up to you. You may appoint a neutral chairperson, or conduct the session yourself, or invite another member of the group to do so. At the meetings you should aim to fulfil the basic principles of:

1   producing a progress report (which may be transformed, or incorpo-rated, into the final report), specifying what has been achieved and what is still to be done;
2   organising the evidence to support the claims you make in the report;
3   offering your own critical analysis of your work, for example, by show-ing the relationship of the evidence to the claims, or by asking advice about aspects of the work.

When we speak about reaching agreement, what forms of agreement exist, and what is needed for the claim to knowledge to be legitimated?

It would be pleasant, but surprising, if everyone agreed with you. You are not aiming for consensus, though. We are all entitled to our different opinions. Diversity in opinion and critical engagement are characteristics of open societies.

You are looking for confirmation that you have done what you say you have done. You are also looking for feedback about whether or not you are justified in claiming that your intervention has led to improvement of some kind. If your validation group feel that it has not, you would expect them to offer advice about what else you might try.

How many people should agree that your research is to be validated? The validation group will need to establish their own procedures here, through discussion of their responsibilities as assessors, as well as discussion of your work. What happens if no one agrees with you? Then you would need seriously to reflect on what has been said, and aim to re-present your evidence later in such a way that it might shed new light. Remember that you are aiming to influence lives through your research. If you stand by your convictions, be sure you are prepared to accept responsibility for your actions. Be honest about whether you have the best interests of others at heart, and are not simply serving your own.

If your group agree that you have done what you claim to have done, and therefore that your claim to knowledge is a valid claim, you are entitled to proceed in your chosen direction with confidence. Your work has stood the test of critical scrutiny, and you have achieved your goals with integrity.

The following is a briefing sheet produced by Pam, while she was Professor of Educational Research, for validation meetings in the MA programme at Kingston University. You could adapt it to suit your needs in your own validation processes.

BRIEFING SHEET

Purpose

The purpose of the validation meeting is for action researchers to test out their claims to have managed change in their professional practice by presenting evidence to a sympathetic but critical audience. The result of a successful meeting should be for the researcher to have an enhanced understanding of the research and a clearer idea of its direction.

Role of validation group

The validation group should comprise:

- the tutor
- members of the support set
- a critical friend(s)
- an independent person from another support set

(Opportunity should be made for a small number of first-year students to observe the meeting. The course director may attend some meetings.)

continued on next page

Validators should have access to the relevant information prior to the meeting in the form of a short report. Their role is to look carefully at the evidence, listen to the account given by the researcher, probe through questioning and finally to contribute to the evaluation of the evidence in relation to the claims being made. Their role is that of sympathetic critic rather than unconditional supporter!

Preparation for meeting

Researchers must have the *agreement of the tutor* before they proceed to validation. The tutor is responsible for checking that the claims to be made are sufficient and clear enough to support a dissertation at Master's level.

A short report (one to two pages) setting out the context and aims of the research should be prepared for the validation group and circulated a day or so before the meeting. It could be in the form of the original proposal, i.e.:

- What was my concern?
- What were the reasons for my concern?
- What did I do about it?
- What are the outcomes?

It should include a list of the claims that will be made.

Evidence to support the claims should be presented at the meeting. Meetings should not be held until the researcher has sufficient evidence to support claims.

The meeting

The meeting should last about one hour. The researcher should document what is said carefully. Tape-recording is useful. An account of the validation meeting should go in the dissertation as an appendix.

Assessment

The validation meeting and the documentation that accompany it are part of the *assessment process*.

continued on next page

1   In order for the researcher to *proceed* to the next stage of the research the validation group should be satisfied that the claims being made are supported by the evidence and that the researcher is on the right track. If the group wishes to *recommend* that the researcher follow a particular course of action it should be clearly specified on the validation record.

2   Where the claims are not supported by the evidence but the researcher demonstrates a clear understanding of the steps to be taken to close this gap, the researcher may *proceed* but with the expectation that *conditions* are met. These conditions must be specified clearly on the back of the validation record. In the event of changed circumstances, where the conditions are no longer appropriate, the researcher must obtain the agreement of the tutor to a change of direction and this must be recorded on the validation record.

3   Where the researcher does not produce evidence to support the claims or where the claims themselves need major revision, the researcher must not proceed but *repeat the validation*. The regulations allow for the validation to be repeated on one occasion only.

At the end of the validation meeting the validation record should be completed and signed by the group. The tutor should ensure that the researcher has a copy to include in the dissertation and that the course director has a copy of the validation record and other papers for assessment purposes.

At the beginning of this chapter we said that issues of claims to knowledge, validity claims, evidence, criteria, standards of judgement and legitimation processes are all part of the same field. Central to validation is the setting of appropriate criteria by which data may be turned into evidence, and the standards of judgement used in doing so. These issues, as well as the politics of legitimation processes, are dealt with in Chapter 10.

Chapter 10

Criteria, standards of judgement and legitimation processes

This chapter contains the following sections:

- Contemporary debates
- Criteria for judging action research
- In legitimation processes, who is entitled to speak and be listened to, and who decides?

The chapter deals with some of the problematics involved in debates around which criteria and standards of judgement are appropriate in making judgements about validity, and how they are used. These issues are problematic because they are always politically influenced. Making judgements about good quality involves the negotiation of value judgements, because the idea of 'good' is value laden, and what is 'good' for one person is not necessarily so for another. Legitimation is also a value-laden political act, and depends on issues such as:

- Who is making the judgement?
- What criteria does that person use in making the judgement?
- What standards of judgement does that person use?
- Who decides who is entitled to make judgements?

To appreciate some of the dilemmas involved, and how these might impact on your research, it is important to be familiar with some contemporary debates around these issues.

Contemporary debates

In historical terms, action research is still new, and only beginning to become a recognised tradition. There is still scepticism from some people working in established traditions about whether action research should be recognised as 'real' research. This is particularly evident in debates about criteria, because different standards of judgement are used in setting criteria.

Even as recently as the 1990s, issues of legitimation were deeply contested. It was still widely assumed that the old scholarship criteria of generalisability and replicability were the criteria by which research projects should be judged. The traditional criteria for report writing would still apply to new scholarship work. For example, if an academic report did not have a literature review, it would fail. It was also a concern that the number of people qualified to act as examiners in formal settings was quite limited. These matters are now becoming resolved, with new generations of action researchers coming through, and the emergence of a new knowledge base comprising their reports, dissertations and theses. These documents are available increasingly through the conventional media of books and scholarly papers, as well as through the electronic media of websites. New generations of researchers contain people who will become the examiners of the future. The growing bodies of literature explain how research projects might be judged in terms of new, academically approved, types of criteria. The knowledge base does need strengthening, however.

The battles are far from over, and new problematics are emerging. In the Introduction we authors expressed our concerns that in some quarters action research is being regarded as a new technical form of activity that requires practitioners to perform in specified ways. Researchers are expected to produce 'results', and their research is assessed accordingly. If this continues to be the case, the world of education research will not advance significantly from the old scholarships. Therefore it is imperative that new dissertations and theses continue to contribute to the knowledge base, to show how outcomes may be understood as learning, not performance, and how validation processes should work in relation to the values of improved living rather than technical performance.

How are criteria identified, and what standards of judgement are used?

Criteria are the signs by which something is judged. People set criteria in terms of what they understand as 'good'; that is, their values. Criteria vary with the people who select them. People working in corporations might

set criteria that are different from those set by, say, parents, or practitioners working in informal education settings. Corporations might judge
the value of work experience as cultivating values around the accumulation of profit, while parents and practitioners might do so in terms of
the development of life choices. The criteria which people choose are
informed by the standards they consider important for judging the quality
of life.

Some people maintain that there are universal standards, for example,
that music can be judged in terms of specific criteria. Other people would
say that appreciation of music is a personal experience. One person
might love classical music, another pop music. Both are 'right', because
they have identified their own preference and can justify their choice in
terms of what they choose. There are no overarching standards of judgement to call on. Each field of experience is particular to the people
involved, and they negotiate what is worthwhile in their context according
to their own aesthetic values. However, power often intrudes, and in real-
life experiences, particularly formal organisational life, the most powerful
voices determine what counts as 'good', and therefore what criteria and
standards of judgement apply.

You need to be aware of these issues, because in many ways, particularly if you are in a formal setting, you are in a complex game and you
need to be aware of the rules of the game if you wish your project to be
judged successful. The idea of being in a game is not cynical. Social situations are highly sophisticated and regulated by particular rules. If you obey
the rules, you will probably have a quiet life. If you are disobedient, you
may be in for troublesome times.

If you are doing research without aiming to present it in a public forum,
you can basically do as you please, but your research would not then conform to the notion of systematic enquiry that is taken as a major criterion
of research. If your work is to be regarded as legitimate research, it must
be made public. In informal settings, this means making your work available to colleagues, but you would not expect any kind of formal award for
your work. In an academic setting, it would imply that you were making
a formal claim to knowledge and were expecting validation in the form
of credit or an award. If your work is part of an award-bearing course,
you do need to abide by the rules of the academic game, although those
rules are changing due to the efforts of creative and courageous people
who constantly push the boundaries and manage to negotiate their
own criteria from within the academic context, using new standards of
judgement.

Because this is such an important issue for those in formal education
settings, where old scholarships are in many places transforming into
new scholarships, it is worth spelling out what kinds of difficulties
remain, and how these are becoming resolved.

Old scholarship criteria

Although things are changing, the situation remains for many that:

- Work is often judged on the technical quality of the report rather than the quality of the practice that the report describes. The set pattern of report writing can be considered more important than accounts of real-life practice.
- While the generic criteria for report writing maintain that the report demonstrates originality of mind and critical judgement, these criteria can be variously interpreted. In old scholarship, 'critical judgement' would take the form of, say, documentary analysis of a literature review. In new scholarship approaches, researchers would use the literature against which to test their own emergent theories.
- The predetermined criteria of examiners are considered more important than the negotiated criteria of practitioners. Therefore the work may be judged in terms quite different from those that the practitioner intended.
- Reports are sometimes judged by examiners who hold different values from the researcher. Examiners might expect to read of an improvement in the external situation. When concrete 'results' are not reported, the work might be considered inadequate. Researchers however might consider that showing an improvement in the quality of their own learning is sufficient.

These dilemmas are well summed up in a classic article by Pam Lomax (1994b). She and colleagues have shown the benefit of supporting practitioners to negotiate their own criteria, while recognising the problems this can raise within traditional academic settings.

New scholarship criteria

- New scholarship criteria emphasise the quality of the researcher's learning as much as situational outcomes. In fact, if the research does not go as planned, and if the researcher can show that they have learnt through dealing with the situation, that is sufficient.
- The report shows the process of personal professional learning. This may be expressed through demonstrating how the researcher took stock of a particular situation, reflected on what they might do, and took appropriate action in order to make a claim that they had improved their practice.
- The criteria of the researcher are expressed in terms of the values they hold. The research focuses on the extent to which these values were lived out. Reasons are given why they were realised, or not.

- Reports are judged by the degree of demonstration of originality and creativity of mind and critical judgement. This refers to how researchers use existing theories in the literature to help move forward their own thinking in enabling them to create their own theory of education.

Criteria for judging action research

It is useful to set criteria at every step of your project. Plan your steps in terms of the action plan outlined on page 60. Here are some ideas about how you might begin, which include and add to those questions, and about the kinds of criteria you could identify that are going to help you decide whether or not the action has been successful. Remember that you can amend these ideas for your own use, and also set your own criteria for judging the quality of your research. This section draws on work undertaken by Pam Lomax at Kingston University.

Step 1
Identifying a concern: What is your research interest (concern)? Why are you interested (concerned)?

Intention for the research: what do you hope to do?

- The action research addresses an issue you have identified in your practice with a view to making changes.
- This is focused into a question of the kind, 'How do I improve my practice of education here?'
- As well as seeking answers to this question you will be exploring the underlying meaning of the question itself.

Rationale: why are you undertaking the research?

- Explain why your concern is professionally relevant and sufficiently important to involve your personal engagement and commitment.
- Providing your rationale will help you to identify your personal professional values, and show any ambiguities or contradictions in relation to your own prejudices or organisational constraints.

Success criteria: how will you make professional judgements about your work?

- You explain the research context.
- You identify and provisionally formulate a research question in terms of 'How do I . . .?'
- You give a rationale. You may well develop this rationale as the research proceeds and the reasons for undertaking the research become clearer.

Step 2
Action planning: what can you do about your interest/concern?

Planning: what do you plan to do?

- Translate the initial intention into a manageable plan. Start small, and see how it develops.
- Aim to establish a clear link between why you want to act and what you do then (between your values and your actions). Try to develop strategies that help you to reflect critically.
- Learn to step back from the action and ask critical questions, such as 'Why am I doing this? What do I hope to achieve?'

Strategies: how will you do this?

- Start with a clear plan of action that includes possible strategies for addressing your research question.
- Be prepared to modify this plan as the research progresses. Try to keep a detailed record of how your intentions become clearer as you proceed.
- Begin to identify where your practice possibly contradicts the values that you claim to hold, and how you might resolve these dilemmas.

Success criteria: how will you make professional judgements about your work?

- Link between reflection and action established.
- Research process made transparent.
- Demonstration of values in practice

Step 3
Involving others: how do you involve others so that your research is collaborative?

Collaborative intent: who will you work with?

- Work to involve colleagues as co-researchers rather than research subjects.
- Encourage colleagues to share your educational experience by doing their own research.
- Involve a colleague such as your critical friend and ask for critical feedback.
- Be prepared to relinquish your ownership of the action when colleagues are ready to take it over.

Your own role: how will you work with them?

- Be open. The integrity of action research depends on not manipulating others.
- Be ready to take risks and possibly expose others to risk.
- Consider the part others play in your research and establish clear ethical principles to guide your research.

Success criteria: how will you make professional judgements about your work?

- Research role made transparent.
- Collaborative intent realised.
- Ethical principles developed and applied.

Step 4
Taking action: how will you gather data to show the situation as it is?

Action: what will you do, and how will you keep track?

- Carefully describe the action you take, including the relationship between events as well as the events themselves.
- Be systematic about monitoring. Collect a variety of data. Try to sample many viewpoints about the same event in order to get a more comprehensive description.
- Sort and store the data carefully to use for further reflection, and to generate evidence for authenticating your research.

Analysis: how will you make sense of what you do?

- In order to make sense of the action, interrogate the data regularly and begin to identify emerging patterns and themes. These patterns and themes are the first steps in creating your own educational theory that is grounded in the events you describe and your experience of them.
- Explain how you have grouped and sorted the data, and what alternatives existed.

Success criteria: how will you make professional judgements about your work?

- Comprehensive data collected from different sources.
- Patterns and contradictions appreciated.
- Analysis exposed to critique.
- Alternatives considered.

Step 5
Evaluation: How will you ensure that any judgements you come to are reasonably fair and accurate?

Evaluation: how will you show that your work was worthwhile?

- Are the outcomes of the research significant? For whom and why? Are you satisfied with these outcomes, or would you have expected others?
- Has there been a practical change in the situation? Can it be justified as educational change? How?
- Have you developed professionally? Can you describe and explain the process of your own learning?
- Does the research have integrity in relation to how you demonstrate ethical awareness?

Validating claims: how will you establish the authenticity of your work?

- Have you made transparent the assumptions and contradictions of your claims to knowledge?
- Is the evidence to support your analysis and explanations sufficient and appropriate?
- Are your claims authentic for your colleagues?
- Can you use your findings as part of critical professional debates?

Success criteria: how will you make professional judgements about your work?

- Claims are shown to be important and relevant.
- Explanations are convincing and authenticated.
- Individual findings are related to critical professional discussion.
- Further questions are generated.

Step 6
Modification of practice: how do you modify your practice in light of your evaluation?

Modification: what are you doing differently?

- Can you explain how you might have done your research differently, and possibly with different outcomes?
- How will you use your evaluation to inform future directions for your work?
- How will you show that the possible new directions will be an improvement on past practice? How do you understand improvement? Have your understandings changed?
- Can you show how your educative influence has helped others also to change their practice? Have you hopes that this wider improvement will lead to possible organisational development?
- How might you manage the next cycle of your action research?

Planning new actions: what might you do in the future?

- Have you decided on new research plans? Why? Can you outline them?
- How will you use your previous findings in your new research? Have you made this explicit?
- Will you move your research into new contexts, perhaps to inform policy issues? How will you do this?
- How will you aim to extend the range of your influence? How will you involve others?

Success criteria: how will you make professional judgements about your work?

- Links established between present findings and future practice.
- Clarification of understanding of what educational improvement entails.
- New action plans outlined that show how learning is incorporated.
- Explanations offered for extending the range of educative influence.

Step 7
Making public: how do you disseminate your findings?

Reporting: how will you make your work publicly available?

- Who will read your report? Do they know the criteria they will use to judge it?
- Have you followed the guidelines for the presentation of the report (see Chapter 12)?
- Is your account succinct yet comprehensive?
- A chronological account is important, but it is also important to show the often chaotic experience of doing the research.
- Are the style and language of the report appropriate for the audience?
- Have you written the report in a reader-friendly way?

Making explicit: how will you reflect critically on your own potential contribution?

- Have you clarified the purpose of your report? Who are you, and what was your research about?
- Does the account demonstrate a high standard of awareness of the criteria listed in this section?
- Have you drawn conclusions and subjected these to a critical dialogue drawing upon other sources?
- Have you given sufficient information for readers to follow up leads and check out your information?

Success criteria: how will you make professional judgements about your work?

- The report has clear frames of reference, is well structured, and is jargon-free and user-friendly.
- The report presents a succinct yet comprehensive account that describes the strengths and limitations of the research.
- The implications of the research are spelt out and evaluated critically in relation to other sources of information. The report provides sufficient information for readers to follow up issues that are of interest.

Remember that the above are offered as ideas and starting points for you to use in validating your research. You should aim to build on these ideas and produce your own that are relevant to your area of study. Work with others in critiquing your initial ideas, and develop them collaboratively.

In legitimation processes, who is entitled to speak and be listened to, and who decides?

In any field of human action there are those who speak and who are listened to, and those who do not speak and who are not listened to. This goes against the values of social justice. In situations like these, it is important to try to establish three things as preliminaries for social change:

1   What has happened in the past that has led to the situation?
2   What is happening now that perpetuates the situation?
3   What may be done to change it?

You can do nothing about (1); you can do something about (2), even if doing something about (2) means improving your understanding of (1); and (3) you can decide to improve your understanding and take action. This implies that you would begin exploring issues about who decides who should speak and who should be listened to, and who agrees that they have the authority to make those kinds of decisions. These are very difficult issues, and involve understanding the nature of power and how power is distributed in societies.

Power is not a 'thing'; it is within the relationships among people. Some people regard themselves as in power, and they go to elaborate lengths to persuade others that this is the case. Often their systems of persuasion have the desired effect; other people go along with the script, not questioning it, or even thinking that it could be changed. There is a general assumption that this is the way things are because this is the way things are. People already in power continue to make the rules that will keep them there; they get themselves into power and then become the gatekeepers of rule-making procedures as well. They use many overt and covert strategies to control the thinking of others, including intimidation, marginalisation and flattery. Consequently, the general public become dumbed down and obedient, and many are persuaded not only to conform, but not even to see that they are conforming, or question that there might be other, better ways. These processes happen everywhere in societies. Critique is systematically factored out of private and public conversations, and uniformity, complacency and acceptance settle in. This is true of education in all its contexts, a particularly worrying circumstance, given that education is one of the most powerful forces for personal and social improvement.

The situation applies to you and your research project as much as it does to international affairs, especially if you are in a formal academic context. Although massive shifts are currently taking place in the knowledge base of educational enquiry, there are still deeply contested issues about who should know, and who should be regarded as a legitimate knower. Many people in institutions of higher education still do not regard practitioners as legitimate knowledge creators, nor do they regard practitioner-based enquiry as a valid form of theory generation. The increasing number of validated dissertations and theses are challenging the traditional knowledge base, and showing practitioner research to be legitimate, especially in terms of how it relates to and has relevance for social and institutional reform, but there is still a long way to go.

Immediate implications for you are that you need to check in advance what is necessary for your work to be approved. If you are part of an established award-bearing course, the chances are that precedents have now been established, and you have nothing to worry about. If you are in a new scenario, especially if you are involved in doctoral work, you do need to check. Before you submit your work at any point in the validation processes, check your audience and their expectations. Clarify which criteria and standards of judgement are going to be used in assessing it. Check whether or not you have any say in negotiating these criteria. If not, there is little you can do, other than play by the established rules and wait until you are in a position to work towards negotiating what counts as the rules. If you are able to negotiate, you will be able to negotiate your own criteria. This will probably also apply to the form of representation of your report, in which case it is up to you to justify why you have chosen to present your work as a conventional written report, or by another means, such as a video presentation. Much work these days uses multimedia technology for data-gathering and validating processes, and some theses are presented using the same multimedia technologies. Newer criteria are being used (such as those outlined on page 145) that emphasise processes of learning as much as behavioural outcomes. Does the work show the processes of learning involved? Does it show the development of critical reflection? Does it constitute an original contribution which demonstrates creativity of mind and critical engagement? If you are in a situation that allows negotiation, give your examiners guidance about what they should look for in your work, and explain how the work should be validated.

Some of these ideas would not be acceptable to many people working in educational and organisational settings. The values we authors hold in writing them include a commitment to the ideas that people can think, speak and act for themselves, that we all hold an infinitude of knowledge and are capable potentially of acting on it. We believe that each and every person is entitled to make his or her contribution to public debates and should be listened to respectfully. We celebrate diversity in ways of knowing, and we do not privilege certain forms of knowledge because of the power structures that support them. Our work, and the work of those in networks we support, shows how these values are being realised in practice (see http://www.actionresearch.net and http://www.jeanmcniff.com).

In our publications, we present the work of people who have completed their action research dissertations and theses, and we comment critically on the criteria and standards that were judged appropriate for these. Those reports, and the critical conversations around them, show how we are aiming to live out our values as providers and supporters, by enabling people to speak for themselves and show how their contribution has improved the quality of educational experience for themselves and others. Throughout this book we have aimed to offer justification for our work and the values that inform our work, and we hope that we demonstrate our own responsibility in accounting for ourselves. We do not require you to accept these values; you are free to make your own choices. We caution that if you do decide to commit yourself to investigating your practice as the first step in a long process of social change, things may become uncomfortable. You could be going against established norms and creating new ones, and this can be a risky business. However, the risks are worthwhile in terms of the contribution you can make to human flourishing.

Our advice at this stage of your research is to be aware of the risks, and balance out your options. If you choose to fight battles, be selective about what kind of battle it is, and make sure you have powerful allies, such as a tutor who will support you and other sympathetic colleagues who will lend comfort when the going gets rough. Aim for conciliation; that is, conciliation; of people rather than of issues. Try to engage people in conversation. Do not set out to score points. Be wise. Also be courageous. Stand up for what you believe in. People will admire you for your integrity even if they disagree with your ideas. You know who you are and what you can do. Make sure your voice is heard in the world.

Part VI

Going public

Many people are anxious about the idea of going public. They immediately think that this means publishing their work in journals. This is not the case. The ways in which you can go public range from sharing your work with others, such as your critical friends and your validation group, to writing books and appearing on TV.

Sharing the work is vital. Throughout this book we have emphasised that going public is an integral part of the research process, because it is important that your findings and claims are not perceived simply as your opinion, or that your research has been approved because you are popular. The purpose of sharing your work is to invite critique, so that the work can be seen as having been subjected to critical scrutiny, and to have credibility in a wider forum.

Making your work public can take different forms, depending on your context. In informal contexts, even though it is sufficient to present your work to friends and colleagues, you still have to go through the validation procedures outlined so far in order to have the work judged as research and not opinion. In formal contexts you would have to present your work in a more rigorous way.

Chapter 11 focuses on presenting your work in informal contexts. Chapter 12 gives advice about presenting your work in more formal organisational and academic contexts.

Chapter 11

Sharing your research: creating your own living educational theory

In this chapter we discuss how you can share your research and create your own living educational theory, and so contribute to the wider knowledge base of education research. The chapter is in two parts:

- The importance of sharing your work
- Creating your own living educational theory

The importance of sharing your work

The purpose of sharing your work is so that people can learn from it and adopt or adapt your ideas to their own situations, both in terms of its subject matter and also in terms of the enquiry processes. Here are some of the people with whom you may share your work and the places where you may do so.

People in your workplace

The most obvious people with whom to share your research are your work colleagues. They already know that you are doing research, and you have kept them informed, because you did not want to be discourteous, and also because you wanted to avoid being seen as doing something 'unusual'. Many people may already perceive the value of what you are doing and want to learn from it themselves. They may even want to begin their own action research. Others may be indifferent.

Check with your principal or manager about how to make your research accessible to others in your workplace. Perhaps you could make a copy of the final report available, or you may ask for time at a staff meeting, or circulate a memo. If this sounds too much, ask your manager to say publicly that your work is available for anyone who cares to read it, and they should contact you for a copy. Be open about your research, so that professional learning is seen as part of normal practice and not mysterious or 'clever'.

Often action researchers find that they set precedents for collaborative learning in their workplaces, especially if they can show the relevance of what they are doing to improving the quality of workplace life. It is not unusual to find networks of colleagues within the same organisation working collaboratively on individual as well as group projects (e.g. Hewitt, 1994). Often managers will support any work that may improve the organisation, with funding or remitted time, or in another way. These research communities can build a real atmosphere of collegiality in the workplace, much to the benefit of others.

People outside your workplace

Let other people outside the immediate workplace know about your research. Perhaps CEOs, regional and branch managers, and continuing professional development organisers may be interested. Send them a copy of your report, and say that you would be happy to talk about your work with them.

Often organisations have wider networks, particularly if there are special interest groups. Professional development centres can act as meeting places. Aim to join these groups. They often have their own newsletters and e-mail networks. They also organise conferences of their own, and host discussion groups. You would stand a better chance of meeting influential people here than in large organisations. Start small, and see how it develops.

If there is no existing network, it is easy enough to start one. Begin by organising a social evening (negotiate the use of facilities from a sympathetic manager somewhere). Aim to produce a newsletter and get others to contribute. This will mean chasing people for material, so be aware and be good humoured. It is also easy to begin an electronic discussion forum. This can be productive and easy to manage. If you are not brilliant at technology yourself, connect with someone who is, and let them know how valuable they are as a provider, as well as a discussant. E-mail is tremendously valuable in bringing and keeping people together, and a great source of collaborative learning.

Find opportunities to share your work with a wider community. This may be in local or regional centres, or head offices. Make contact with managers, and ask them about any opportunities for you to present your work.

Aim to access national networks and organisations. These give you opportunities to network with people from a wide range of contexts. Conferences and meetings keep you up to date with the best work and sustain your own enthusiasm. They also give you the opportunity to present to a wider audience and raise your own profile (which adds to the importance of your work), as well as to share ideas with an extended public.

Where to present your work

Go to conferences and meetings. This is one of the best ways of gaining further legitimacy and credibility for yourself and your work. It also raises your profile as a researcher, and in most contexts gives added prestige to your organisation. Those organisations that depend on funding from publications would probably support you financially if you were presenting a paper.

Conferences can help you to do the following.

Meet other people

Social occasions at conferences can be the best time to meet researchers from other institutions and contexts. These contacts can be enormously valuable, both in learning about what other people are doing, and also in inspiring new ideas for yourself.

Keep up to date

Listening to top people in the field helps you to keep up to date with new ideas and developments, as well as to get a feeling for new areas of interest or debate within a particular field.

Generate new ideas

The buzz around conferences tends to spark off new ideas. Take your notebook everywhere. Write down only keywords or points from lectures. Your notes can lead to new lines of thought. Many researchers write papers in skeleton form at conferences, picking up ideas from others. This does not mean that it is permissible to use other people's ideas without referencing them, simply that listening to others can spark off ideas in your own mind. *Never* tape-record a presentation without the speaker's permission, and don't get cross if it is denied.

Learn how to write papers

Writing papers can be one of the best exercises for focusing the mind and clarifying for yourself what is important in your research. Don't expect to write the paper in one go. Really good papers take about ten drafts, often more, to final completion. The discipline of the refining and editing process forces you to synthesise in a way that gives sense to the whole. It also ensures that you write for an audience, and not only for yourself (see Chapter 12).

Learn how to present papers

Presenting papers is part of the discipline of bringing coherence to and making sense of your work. Presenting your work as a paper makes you organise your material for other people. Responding to questions forces you to address issues you may not have thought about before, and also helps you to see the value of your work for other people. Watch good presenters. See how they relate to an audience, respond to questions, use technology, generally conduct themselves. Model yourself on the best.

Raise your own profile

There is always a regular group of people who attend conferences. You would become known in a surprisingly short time, especially if you gave a paper. The intellectual stimulation and fellowship of these contacts can be good for your own morale, as well as providing the support and conversational community that all serious researchers need.

Present your paper

Most organisations ask you to send in a proposal or abstract. This is usually reviewed. Getting a paper accepted is far from easy in some cases. The rigorous process does, however, show that your work is valued by peer professionals. Your abstract often goes into the conference programme, so regard it as part of the business of writing the paper, and write a good one. Other people know you first by what you write.

Make the presentation

Rehearse beforehand. Present your paper with care. Never read the paper to an audience; this can be boring and frustrating for them. Summarise the key points, and write them down as prompts for yourself, in large lettering, on one or two sheets of paper or index cards so that you can speak spontaneously and also keep on track. Put these key points also on OHPs or PowerPoint slides or other visuals to support your presentation. Put them in order beforehand, and number them. Mark up your presentation copy to show when you are going to use them. Be prepared to invest time and effort at this stage. You will thank yourself when you come to present the paper.

Produce your talk as a hand-out or paper for distribution. Decide whether to give this out at the beginning or at the end, and let your audience know. You want them to listen to you, not divert their attention to taking notes. Be careful if you hand out copies of your paper in advance, though. The audience may have read it before you finish talking. Or you may want to refer to it as part of the talk. Lively and engaging presenters who are enthusiastic about what they have to say always capture people's attention.

Stay relaxed and businesslike. Your audience is knowledgeable, so don't talk down (or up), and they are generally interested in what you have to say, so don't expect hostility and be defensive. Tell it as it is, don't put on airs and graces, and be honest and engaging. You can only do your best, which is a great deal.

Use technology

Make sure you are confident around any technology you are using, and make sure it works. Set up well in advance. Avoid fumbling with your OHP or computer while talking through ideas. If the technology fails, stay cheerful and focused. People will still listen to what you have to say.

Deal with questions

At the beginning of your presentation, let your audience know if and when they can ask questions or interrupt, whether during the talk or at the end. If someone asks a question while you are speaking, aim to answer the question briefly, but don't lose track of what you are saying, and don't be intimidated into thinking that you should answer the question if it is not relevant or appropriate. This is your presentation; retain ownership of it.

Acknowledge all questions, and aim to answer as many as possible. If you don't know the answer, say so. People respect honesty. Give concise answers to questions, and don't wander off the point. Stay courteous and friendly throughout. People tend to value the opinions of those they respect, so present your work as something of value, be enthusiastic about it yourself, and others will warm to you and your subject matter.

Creating your own living educational theory

Traditional approaches to theory conform to Richard Pring's (2000) definition of a theory:

> Theory would seem to have the following features. It refers to a set of
> propositions which are stated with sufficient generality yet precision
> that they explain the behaviour of a range of phenomena and predict
> which would happen in the future. An understanding of these propo-
> sitions includes an understanding of what would refute them.
>
> (Pring, 2000: 124–5)

In much empirical research a theory is expressed in terms of a set of deter-
minate relationships between a set of variables to see which verifiable
patterns or regularities can be explained. This means that researchers
test whether one aspect of a situation, the dependent variable, is affected
by another aspect, the independent variable, and they aim to establish a
cause and effect relationship between the variables. They come to conclusions about these relationships (which constitute their findings), make
statements about them, and those statements then come to be regarded
as theory, which goes into the public domain and is regarded as true for
all time. The theory is pronounced a good theory provided it can be
applied to circumstances similar to the situation in which the original
experiments were carried out, so the criteria of replicability and generalisability are held to be the hallmarks of a good theory.

This experimental procedure has come to be known as 'the scientific
method'. Philosophers of science such as Sir Peter Medawar and Sir Karl
Popper have pointed out that there is no such thing as 'the' scientific
method, but the nomenclature is resistant to change, possibly because it
is such a convenient idea. It is widely believed that this is the 'correct'
way of generating 'correct' forms of theory.

There are two basic assumptions underpinning the idea that only
traditional forms of theory are legitimate, and both are equally dangerous
for human flourishing. The first is that there is one correct way to do
research. This way is predetermined and linear, and it produces concrete
results that may be applied to all similar circumstances. The second is
that there is one correct way of thinking. This way leads to certain
answers, the answers are there to be found, and the answers are unproblematic (Berlin, 1998). These assumptions are far from the realities of
human experience. As well as being full of joy and fulfilment, human
experience is also full of anomalies, dilemmas without resolution, trade-
offs, compromise and irremediable disappointment. Human experience
is spontaneous, creative, unpredictable, uncontrollable, and frequently
incomprehensible. Traditional forms of scholarship and theory may be

sufficient to predict and control certain forms of behaviour, but they are inadequate for understanding and explaining how people give meaning to their lives as they live with the glorious muddle. New forms of theory are needed.

Action research is one response to the drive to find new ways of thinking and new forms of theory. When people study their own practice, they produce descriptions (what they did) and explanations (why they did it) of their practice. They act and they reflect, and they act in new ways as their reflections suggest. When they think about what they are doing, they are theorising their practice. In the same way that you can say, 'I have a theory about cats' or 'I have a theory about why people do such and such', so you can also say, 'I have a theory about what I am doing'. If your work is in management education, and you have studied how you have done something differently, you could say, 'I have created my own theory about management' or even 'I have created my own theory of management'. You can create your own personal theory about any aspect of your work, regardless of where that work is located. This theory is a part of you. Because you are a living person, you are changing every day; and because you are reflecting consciously on what you are doing, and making adjustments as you go, your theory is also developing with you. Your theory is part of your thinking, which is in process of transforming all the time. So your theory, as part of your own thinking, is living. You can say you are constantly creating and re-creating your own living theory. If you work in education, or you are concerned about educational matters, you can say that you are creating your own living educational theory.

Jack Whitehead explains his ideas about living educational theories, a term he created, as follows: In living educational theories the explanatory principles are embodied values that have been transformed in the course of their emergence in practice into communicable standards of practice and judgement. In living theories the explanations are not derived from sets of interconnected propositions as in traditional theories. In living educational theories the explanations are produced by practitioner-researchers in enquiries that are focused on living values more fully in the practice of enquiries of the kind, 'How do I improve what I am doing?'

You can find these ideas expressed throughout Jack's writing, available on http:www.actionresearch.net.

Go back to the ideas of validation. In traditional approaches, theory was held to be constituted of verbal statements that are arrived at through analysis of the relationships between variables. The theory was tested when the relationships were demonstrated to conform to accepted norms. It was validated when norms were agreed to have been maintained. In new scholarship approaches, theory is held to be constituted of verbal and non-verbal statements that are arrived at through reflective dialogue about the nature of lived experience. It is tested when the experience can be demonstrated as the grounds for learning and growth, and as having implications for further learning and growth. It is validated when the processes of learning and growth are agreed to have been nurtured.

In new scholarship approaches, theory is tested against other people's experience. To have your theory authenticated as valid, you have to show, through supporting evidence, how and why you have influenced other people in the way you hoped. While the theory exists within you, and is part of you, it is also part of other people, because they contribute to your life and you to theirs. Your theory is manifested in your relationship with other people, and it develops as your relationships develop.

Conclusion

These ideas about the nature of theory and theory generation are exciting and provide opportunities for engaged scholarly debate. Debates about the nature of new scholarship forms of theory will probably never be conclusive, because debates themselves develop the field and generate new forms. Perhaps this is the nub: the new scholarship is about resisting closure, a commitment to re-creation. It is this very commitment to open-endedness that is antipathetic to traditional ways. Traditionalists are secure with certainty and are often threatened by uncertainty, so they attempt to retain certainty about certainty. In many ways it is about how we view life and death, whether life is a forward-looking, living-on-the-brink experience, or a journey towards the end. Each one of us must make our own decisions about this.

Chapter 12 explains the processes of sharing your work through writing it up as a report. Your research report is the synthesis of your action and reflection, and is the articulation of the theory you have generated by studying your practice.

Chapter 12

Producing your report

This chapter looks at the following issues:

- Different ways of communicating using different forms of representation
- Writing reports for different purposes

Now that you have done all the hard work of gathering data and processing it in order to generate valid evidence, you need to present the work in a form that is going to serve your particular purposes as well as represent your work authentically. For most people, this means producing a report which will contain their claim that they have improved their personal professional situation in some way. Before we discuss the different kinds of report you may produce, it is worth considering how different forms of representation may communicate messages for different purposes.

Different ways of communicating using different forms of representation

Old and new scholarships create and communicate different kinds of knowledge in different ways, so they usually use different forms of representation.

Traditional scholarships tend to use traditional ways of thinking. The aim is to show how processes of enquiry lead to certain conclusions, and the best way is to use linear forms of thinking and reporting that show the processes of 'If I do this, that will happen'. New scholarships tend to use non-traditional ways of thinking. The aim is to show how processes of enquiry lead to improved practices, and the best way is to use creative ways of thinking and non-linear forms of reporting that show the processes of 'I wonder what would happen if . . .'. Non-linear ways of thinking and forms of reporting can be represented using a variety of media, including writing, story, dialogue, visual and other sensory representation, and a combination of all these forms. Different ways of knowing may be communicated using different forms of representation; we can show how our embodied values become real using a variety of forms. Here are some of them.

Writing

Writing is still the primary form for presenting reports. Newer forms are appearing, such as those using multimedia technology (see the next section). Writing takes many forms and serves many purposes, the most common of which are as follows.

Communicating the processes of thinking

Writing is a valuable way of showing the processes of thinking. Some writers explain how the experience of writing can be a form of thinking and knowledge generation.

> In writing I tap my tacit knowledge. I externalise my thoughts-at-competence through my action-at-performance. My writing becomes both symbolic expression of thought (this is what I mean) and the critical reflection on that thought (do I really mean this?). My writing is both reflection on action (what I have written) and reflection in action (what I am writing). The very act of making external, through the process of writing, what is internal, in the process of thinking, allows me to formulate explicit theories about the practices I engage in intuitively.
>
> (McNiff, 1990: 56)

Representing dialogue

Many researchers use a dialectical way of representing meaning by publishing their authentic conversations that show the processes of the creation of living theories. These conversations show how people talk about the dilemmas and contradictions in their work, and how they were successful, or not, in finding ways through. Some accounts (see e.g. Cahill, 2000; McDermott, 2001) explain that the outcomes of the research are located more in the emergent understandings that are inspired through engaging in those conversations.

Some researchers have experimented with drama as a form of representation. The research story unfolds through the experiences of the persons involved. Using this form, it is possible to communicate both the action of the research as well as a critical commentary of the process. Perselli's (2002a and b) are good examples of reports that use dramatic form. There are also good references to performance text in Mills (2000).

Diaries

Many researchers use extracts from their diaries to communicate the insights generated through the research process. Diary entries are often used as valuable pieces of data. Extensive and systematic use of diaries can show the process itself. Christopher McCormack (2002), for example, uses extracts from his diary both to tell the story and to record his reflections on events.

Story

Story also represents processes of personal enquiry. There is no necessary linear logic of connectedness in story. Even the beginning, middle and end of traditional story have been suspended for the postmodern novel. Stories are generative in the way they encourage diverse and original interpretations both for their authors and their audiences. Moyra Evans' (1993b) use of story is a good example of how a narrative can transform both its author's understanding and also engage others in its development. She adopted an action research approach to facilitating the professional development of staff. After working with a department for a year she presented her data in the form of a fictional story. She wrote the story to be consistent with the values system of the players in the scene, as interpreted by herself, and she negotiated her ideas with those whom the story represented.

Two of the best examples of research as story-telling are Dadds and Hart's (2001) *Doing Practitioner Research Differently*, and Winter and Munn-Giddings' (2001) *A Handbook for Action Research in Health and Social Care* (mentioned already on page 12). Authors use many ways of story-telling to communicate their truths. Joe Geraci (2001, in Dadds and Hart) uses story to explain how an outsider can 'get inside' the experience of another person's autism. Philip Ingram (2001, in Winter and Munn-Giddings) takes another sensitive subject (a close relative suffering from Alzheimer's disease) and uses story to communicate the emotions that the experience evokes. The experience of the reader is probably far more profound through reading these stories than it would have been if a conventional form of reportage had been used. Other excellent works are Overboe (2001) and Bai (2001), both of which show how story enables one to access the meanings that lie beneath cognitive awareness and understand the interconnectedness of mind and body, self and the world.

The use of story as a form of research reporting has been pioneered by researchers such as Jean Clandinin and Michael Connelly, who have developed the traditions of narrative enquiry to a high degree (see Clandinin and Connelly, 2000).

Poetry

Many researchers use poetry to represent the experiences of doing the research and the understandings that emerge. Poetry can communicate well the idea of how embodied values emerge as lived realities.

Patchwork approaches

Richard Winter (see Winter *et al.*, 1999) has pioneered the idea of using a 'patchwork' approach. He encourages researchers to use a combination of techniques, such as critical fictional writing, poetry, drama and traditional reporting, to show the different research phases and the kinds of understanding they generate.

It has to be said that these novel ways of representing research would probably have been frowned upon by some researchers as recently as the 1990s. However, many precedents have been set by courageous researchers for whom the process of doing the research, and representing it authentically, was often more important than the award they received. Because these researchers also maintained traditional high standards of rigour and went through stringent validation procedures, their research was approved, and these reports have now established innovative forms of representation as part of the new traditions of the new scholarship.

Multimedia approaches

These may well still be termed 'audiovisual' approaches, but the more innovative versions tend to involve whole-body engagement, representing different ways of knowing. Different ways of knowing can best be explicated using different forms of representation. This can be done using a variety of technologies that show the creative, non-linear processes of coming to know.

Visual representation

Some researchers have developed innovative ways of communicating life experiences. Zoe Parker (1993), for example, uses snake charts; that is, curved lines that have marked on them at intervals the epiphanies of the research process: key moments, ideas or people that have had significant impact. Mary McDaniel (2002) asked her groups of nurse practitioners to communicate the insights generated through doing their research by drawing what their situation was like before they began their enquiries, and then to produce visuals at specified points during the process to communicate the development of ideas and insights. Mary Roche teaches children to develop higher order thinking skills. In her (2000) Master's dissertation she recounts how she invited the children to draw pictures of their own ideas, and to explain, orally and in writing, why these pictures showed how their thinking was developing. Miriam McGuire-Shelley (2000) involves children in exploring their own sense of connectedness through multiple sensory representations.

Many researchers use charts and diagrams to communicate the processes of doing the research. These visual metaphors can be powerful, and communicate well the values that inform the research processes as well as the forms of methodologies involved. Jean McNiff's visual on page 28 communicates her ideas of the generative transformational nature of open-ended enquiries. The visual is informed by the values of freedom and the creative nature of knowledge. In current work she is exploring the idea of the potential evolution of evolvability. Geoff Mead (2001) uses metaphor to show the unfolding of meaning through question and dialogue. When we use these written and visual metaphors to guide our work, however, it is important to remember that the metaphor remains a metaphor. In doing the work we go beyond the metaphor, and show the living reality of how we aim to realise our values in our practices. Bourdieu's (1990) ideas are instructive here, when he speaks about how some people confuse the reality of the model with the model of reality. Metaphors are valuable ways of coming to know, but it is then crucial to communicate what we know, and leave the metaphor behind.

Multimedia representations

Wonderfully creative work is being undertaken by some researchers to show how different technologies can communicate different ways of thinking. Traditional ways of knowing (epistemologies) use traditional forms of representation. They emphasise cognitive, rational processes. These forms tend to work towards closure, because rational processes work on the assumption that unambiguous answers to everything are waiting to be discovered, and these answers can be arrived at by the rational processes of inductive analysis. New epistemologies assume that people come to know through their whole bodies, not only their brains. Researchers such as Howard Gardner (1983) have developed these ideas into a theory of multiple intelligences. In this theory, people come to know through all their senses – visually, kinaesthetically and emotionally, as well as linguistically and numerically. Knowing is a personal whole-body experience. The knowledge created at a personal level can be developed intrapersonally through self-reflection, and interpersonally through dialogue with others.

Researchers who find these views meaningful for their own lives are building on the seminal work of Gardner and others, and finding new ways of communicating embodied ways of knowing as much as cognitive ways of knowing. As well as the written forms outlined above, they are exploring the use of multimedia technologies that show how knowledge is created through the personal experimental use of computers, and how their personal knowledge is then developed through dialogue which can take place through the facilitating media of information and communication technologies (ICTs). Innovators in the field include Jack Whitehead (http:ww.actionresearch.net), Margaret Farren (http://www.compapp. dcu.ic/umforren) and Máirín Glenn (http://www.iol.ie/~belmullets). Jack's work as a professional educator focuses on how he can support practitioners' enquiries as well as co-ordinate practitioner networks around the world to enable people to share and develop their enquiries, and in so doing build a coherent knowledge base for new forms of scholarship (see e.g. Whitehead and DeLong, 2003). Margaret's work as a professional educator focuses on how she can support educators using multimedia technologies. Máirín's work as a classroom teacher focuses on how she can help children develop their multiple ways of knowing through the creation of the kinds of dialogical spaces that multimedia technologies allow. Another valuable website to access is that of Sandra Weber and Claudia Mitchell at http://www.iirc.mcgill.ca.

This kind of work is still in its infancy. Its enormous potentials are waiting to be explored, but they promise rapid future developments that will bring action enquiries into new dimensions. These new forms of representation are becoming accepted as part of higher degree work. The work is innovative, and much has yet to be done.

Writing reports for different purposes

This section focuses on the more traditional and established forms of written reports. It offers general guidelines on the kind of reports you may write, as well as how to write them.

Writing a research report requires a clear and concise presentation. It is important to remember that reports are written for a reader. They are not written for the author. It is the author's responsibility to make sure that the report can be read easily and fluently, and that frequent signposts are provided to guide the reader. If readers are expected to guess what the report is saying, or to read between the lines, they will probably not read it.

What goes into the report depends on its purpose and on the audience who will read it. These two factors determine the style of writing and the content. The writing and content would be different, for example, if a report is written for colleagues, a tutor or an academic audience. Different contexts also influence what is written and how it is written. Newspaper articles are shorter and more concise than, say, a professional newsletter, and dissertations are longer and more detailed than a paper for an academic journal.

Whichever forum you are writing for, you need to decide the following:

What is the content?

All action research reports have in common some specifications concerning content. These include traditional considerations such as linking theory and practice, contextualising the work, showing regard for good ethical practice, relating the work to the literature, and drawing justified conclusions. They also include the new scholarship considerations of showing an improvement in practice and making claims about how this has happened that will help others to learn from the work. This means presenting the report in such a way that it consistently demonstrates methodological and epistemological rigour, as well as convincing the reader of the truth and importance of the learning that has taken place.

How will it be presented?

As well as providing appropriate content, the report has to be organised in a form that meets the conventions of report writing, whether the report is presented in traditional or innovative ways. These include clear signposting to lead the reader, headings to guide attention, clarity of expression, avoidance of jargon, and good language and writing skills.

There are different types of report. Two of the most common are a professional portfolio and a Master's dissertation. Here are some guidelines for writing. The advice given for portfolio work applies also to dissertation work.

A professional portfolio

Portfolio work is usually organised in terms of modules. Institutions have their own requirements for the number of modules that make up the entire portfolio. Portfolio work requires you to present your learning in a coherent way, so that you can be given credit for it that will count towards

. an overall award. The credit is given in terms of professional learning that you feel is worthy of credit (accredited prior learning (APL)) and learning that has been formally accredited by a recognised institution (accredited learning (AL)).[1] Acknowledgement of accredited learning presents few difficulties. You have your certificates which you can submit for credit. If you wish to claim credit for learning that has not been accredited (prior learning), you need to make a case why that learning has been valuable and has contributed to your professionalism.

A wide range of experiences may be relevant to the submission of your portfolio. Take time to consider what episodes of your life may be considered to be professional learning, and make a chronological list. What was special about these episodes? What kind of learning did they generate? Whom did the learning benefit? Can you make a case that this was professional learning which helped your overall development?

When you submit your claim for credit, you need to show both the evidence for the learning, and also give an explanatory framework to show how this learning has influenced your future practice. The evidence will often take the form of other people's testimonies that they have benefited from your educative influence. It is no use submitting only lists of activities: these are descriptions, not explanations, and they say nothing in terms of why you did what you did, or its potential for future development. By providing an explanatory framework for your descriptions, you can locate your evidence within wider issues to explain the reality of your influence in practice.

Explanatory framework

Your explanatory framework will include giving reasons for using a particular methodology (see below). The most common methodological traditions used in portfolio work include autobiography research, which is linked to narrative enquiry, and action research. You may have a particular focus to your work that means you would include other methodologies such as feminist research or policy research.

Autobiography is a way of understanding personal practice by telling one's own story, and identifying critical incidents within that account which prompted a change of direction or a piece of significant learning. In telling how the incident affected your personal and professional life, you can show how it inspired learning that encouraged you to reflect on and possibly change your practice.

---

1 Different nomenclatures exist. Some institutions refer to AP(E)L, the accreditation of prior (experiential) learning. In addition, the term 'accreditation of prior (experiential) learning' is rather confusing, because the learning has not yet been accredited, and is only now being submitted for accreditation.

Action research is a form of enquiry that involves action and research. It is a way that enables you to explain how you came to develop your work as praxis. In this book we have taken the stand throughout that a consideration of values is a necessary starting point for an enquiry that aims to establish the extent to which those values are being realised in practice, and to document systematically how those values begin to emerge in practice as the standards by which we judge what we do and think. The focus on values is consistent.

An overall framework for your portfolio that combines autobiography and action research would be to give a brief overview of your current situation, saying that the purpose of the portfolio would be to document the extent to which you have lived your values in the past. This would involve you showing how previous learning has helped you to develop critical awareness of your own situation, and how you may take action to change it in an educational way.

Form of your report

For each unit, your evidence (reports, certificates and other artefacts) should be framed in a short report. This report represents your claim to knowledge.

The form of the report should communicate the process of self-reflective learning. The following questions provide your necessary framework. They are the same kind of questions we have used throughout this book. You can use these questions, or adapt them to suit your own purposes.

- What did I wish to investigate when I undertook this piece of learning?
- Why did I wish to investigate it?
- How can I show the evidence of what the situation was like at the time?
- What did I think I could do about it?
- What did I do?
- What evidence can I produce to show my actions and their impact?
- What did I learn?
- How can I show my learning?
- How can I evaluate the impact of my educative influence?
- How can I evaluate the impact of this learning on my professional practice?
- How has it extended me as a professional?
- How can I show that I have taken care that any conclusions I have come to are reasonably fair and accurate?
- How have I modified my present practice in the light of past learning?

This framework enables you to tell your story of how you have tried to improve your practice by undertaking a piece of learning which helps you to live in the direction of your educational values.

Presenting your report

Use the same section headings as you used for your action research reports for your outline plan. If you wish you can use the headings given below. You can of course make up headings of your own. Here are some questions that could provide a framework. The headings may be adapted for other reports, such as Master's dissertations (see pages 182–190).

What did you wish to investigate when you undertook this piece of learning?

Contextualise the study. Explain who you were at the time, what the context was, what gave rise to your research issue. Was it a problem? Why? Was it a demonstration of good practice? How? Have you given a description of the practice so that any reader will understand what inspired you to begin your investigation?

Why did you wish to investigate it?

Give a brief statement of your own professional values base. If the situation inspired you to begin taking action to change it, what was it about the situation that needed changing? Was something happening that went against what you believe in? Perhaps the situation was so excellent that you wanted to share the good news by showing how and why the situation was as it was. This would mean you evaluated it, and produced reasons for what was happening.

Throughout this section, try to relate your research issue to the values you hold as a professional, and show what relevance doing the research has had to your professional life. If you are giving an account of the changes you tried to make, make sure you explain why you felt you were justified in taking action. Always discuss the steps you took to ensure whether your perceptions of the situation were accurate. Why could you not tolerate the ambiguity? Why did you not leave well alone? By considering these issues you will show how you were justified in taking the action you did, that it was not just interference, and that you were acting in the interests of a specific value such as social justice. These kinds of issues contribute to your explanations (why you did what you did) and are an important part of your overall explanatory framework.

How can you show the evidence of what the situation was like at the time?

Was there a problem? If so, how would your reader understand what the problem was like? Was it an excellent situation? What picture of the context can you paint? Produce some kind of evidence, using any of the ways outlined on pages 114–128, to show why you felt you wanted to investigate or evaluate it. The main point here is to show your reader what the situation was like and what was happening that inspired you to take action.

What could you do about it?

Spell out what you felt your options were, and any possible solutions. Explain that you consulted with others (if you did) in helping you to decide what to do. There could have been a range of options for you to choose from. Explain why you decided on one course of action to begin with, and also say how you may have developed a different action plan if your first option proved unproductive.

What did you do?

What course of action did you take? Was it straightforward? Did you stick to only the one option, or did you try out several in quick succession? Did you change your mind? Why? What happened?

This section gives an account of your action. Remember that your reader has no idea what you did. Tell the story in a direct way. Say the obvious. Often researchers imagine that the reader will anticipate the most obvious things, because they are so obvious. This is not so. You must state the obvious, even if it seems overkill to do so.

It can help to tell the story into a tape-recorder, or to talk it through with someone else and ask them to tape-record it or make notes as you go along. They will probably say, 'What happened when . . .?' They will check on pieces you may have left out or that are unclear. Telling someone the story can act as your first draft. When you write it down, imagine that you are telling the story all over again to another person.

What evidence did you produce to show your actions and their impact?

Here you need to produce another set of data, which by now you should be turning into evidence by showing the relationship of the data to identified criteria. You will try to establish what influence you may have had on the research situation.

Explain what data-gathering techniques you used. Why did you choose them and not others? What significant features of the data did you select as representative of what you were hoping to achieve? Why these features and not others? Can your reader clearly see your evidence, as well as a statement from you about which criteria you chose to help you make judgements about your practice? Were these criteria linked with your values, as set out earlier in your report?

By this stage you should be producing evidence generated from your data. This could be in the form of fieldnotes, videotape-recordings, transcripts and selections from any other aspect of your data. Put this evidence in the main body of your text. Do not aim to include long pieces of evidence. Short, concise extracts are needed. Place all raw data in the appendices or in your archive as appropriate (see page 109). Here, include only those excerpts from the raw data that will act as evidence to show an improvement in your practice, and possibly in the practices of other people.

What did you learn?

A common error in report writing is to concentrate on the descriptions, but not to document the learning. It is quite easy to write a description of the action. It is difficult to write about your own learning. For example, suppose you tried a different method for chairing meetings. You would describe what you did: you invited J. to chair rather than yourself. What did you learn? Perhaps you learned that people need help to be a successful chair. Perhaps you feel frustrated when people do not do the job as well as you can. Perhaps you have come to appreciate that people have to practise in order to learn, and it is your job to provide opportunities for that learning to take place. You could have learned a multitude of things from this one brief episode. Or suppose you praised someone publicly. You may have learned from this that people shine when praised, that perhaps you do not praise often enough, that there is a relationship between productivity and people's well-being. This kind of reflection on personal learning is at the heart of accounts of good practice.

How can you show that learning?

You can use a variety of techniques for communicating your learning. As you write the description of what you did, you could also weave in an explanation for what you did in terms of your learning. Then descriptions and explanations appear as integrated (as they should). You may choose to write a short reflection after the description. You could use different type fonts to differentiate the descriptions and explanations. You may write the descriptive account under one section heading, and then take a new section to offer explanations in terms of your own reflection and learning. At this point, always aim to include evidence of your own learning – that is, extracts from your data related to the criteria of your values – that you have learned something of value. For example, you could include a diary entry from earlier in your study, and then a current entry, to show the difference in your own thinking. Or you could include a one-minute extract from a video tape to show how you behaved earlier, and then show a second extract to show how your behaviour has changed. This behavioural evidence would have to be backed up by some kind of commentary that stated specifically how you had become aware of changes in your own behaviour and why that may have happened.

To repeat: producing evidence of one's own professional learning is perhaps one of the trickiest aspects of written reports, but it is crucial. It also marks the difference between a report that will pass on adequate merit and a report whose merit is outstanding.

How can you evaluate the impact of your educative influence?

When you speak about your educative influence, you are referring to the extent to which you have influenced people so that they will realise more fully the potentials of their own learning. This implies that you need to evaluate whether or not you have helped people to grow, mentally, physically and spiritually, and to appreciate how they come to grow. You can do this by finding evidence within the lives or accounts of other people to show that they have learned from you how to learn for themselves. This evidence exists throughout your data. In your fieldnotes you may find a note saying how one person appears to have become more confident because you have started spending quality time talking with them about their work; in your tape-recordings someone will have said that they understand their work schedule better because you worked with them in a considerate manner; photographs will show people laughing with you rather than looking glum. All these pieces of evidence, particularly when triangulated (page 69), make up a powerful scenario of your educative influence in the lives of other people, to the extent that the quality of their lives has been improved through their own learning which you have prioritised.

How can you evaluate the impact of the learning on your professional practice?

You are testing how your own systematic reflection and learning about your practice is helping you to understand where you still need to change things. You understand what you are doing well, and you see areas where you still need to adjust. Other issues may also have arisen.

While you feel one aspect of your practice is now satisfactory, this may have revealed other aspects that need urgent attention. The external situation may also have changed that now prompts you to change what you thought was satisfactory. It never stops!

How has it extended you as a professional?

Marks of a professional include care and responsibility to others with whom one is working, expert subject knowledge and personal accountability. By studying your practice, and producing ongoing evaluations, you are demonstrating that you are showing care and responsibility for the welfare of others. You are constantly weighing your decisions in light of what you know and what you still need to know, and you are holding yourself accountable for your actions.

How can you show that you have taken care that any conclusions you have come to are reasonably fair and accurate?

What validation processes did you put in place to support your claim that you were influencing the situation? What changes did you record, both in yourself and in the situation? Who were your validators? Why did you choose them? Did they bring a critical perspective to the process, or could there be a hint of collusion? Where are the accounts of the validation processes? Did you tape-record the meetings, and can these recordings be accessed? Did you ask people to observe you in action, and keep records of their observations? Did you keep your own records? Are you clear that you formulated your criteria in terms of the values that inform your work and inspired you to take action, and can you show that you have fulfilled those criteria by producing evidence? How did people validate your evidence? How can you ensure that anyone reading your report believes that this is an authentic account, and not a piece of fiction?

These are stringent conditions for ensuring that your validation procedures are rigorous and trustworthy. They avoid accusations from people working outside the action research tradition that your work is sloppy or ill-informed or not to be taken seriously. These are still important considerations in what counts as knowledge and who is considered a legitimate knower.

How have you modified your present practice in the light of past learning?

What impact has your study had on your practice? Did you begin doing things differently? Did you decide to continue with the research perhaps from a different perspective? Has your research impacted on your workplace in any way? Can you show that others have adopted new practices because of your influence? Are policies changing because of your findings? Can you show that your work has influenced your own personal development, the professional development of others, and led to changes in wider institutional structures and processes? If so, you can say that your theories have transformed into theories of professional development and organisational change.

Here is an example of the requirements for a professional development module that could contribute to a professional portfolio. It is taken from the Action Research 1 Module in the University of Bath Advanced Courses Programme from October 1995 to 1996, and was developed in Master's programmes at Brock and Bishops Universities in 1999 to 2000 (see http://www.bath.ac.uk/~edsajw/mastermod.shtml).

PREPARING A PROFESSIONAL PORTFOLIO

Purpose

The purpose of this module is to enable participants to carry out an action enquiry, to understand the fundamental principles of action research, and to locate the significance of the approach to institutional, local and national governmental policies.

Organisation

This module will begin by focusing on the participant's understanding of what constitutes an educational enquiry. This will lead into the design of short action enquiries into areas of the participant's own choosing. These enquiries will be carried out over a four- to five-week period, using the group as a peer learning set in which issues and problems related to their enquiry will be addressed and discussed in detail. A final draft of the action enquiry report will then form the basis for participants' self- and peer assessments.

The module will progress in three stages.

Content

1 What constitutes an educational enquiry?

Participants will give examples of educational enquiries drawn from their professional practice. These will be related to examples in the literature on different approaches to action research. The appropriateness of qualitative and quantitative methods for educational enquiries

continued on next page

---

will be discussed (e.g. case study, action enquiry). Participants will then begin to formulate their own personal action enquiry to be carried out during the remainder of the term (this may be an individual or group enquiry).

2 Formulating and carrying out an action enquiry

Participants will present a draft of their action enquiry 'design' which will be the focus for discussion. They will then carry out their enquiry over the next four or five weeks, reporting back to the group on issues and problems arising from their enquiry. This will be the focus for group discussion/analysis/reference to literature and so on. During this time it is envisaged that we will consider the integration of the methods and conceptual frameworks from the disciplines of education into an educational enquiry (e.g. conceptual analysis, theories of learning, the use of autobiography and narrative in the presentation of qualitative research).

3 Final draft of an action enquiry report

Participants will present a final draft of their enquiry report. This will be used to share evidence concerning claims to knowledge which emerge from the enquiries. Questions of validity, justification and rigour will be raised and discussed, as will questions concerning the politics of educational knowledge. The latter will focus on the legitimisation of different conceptions of educational theory from a dialectical perspective. The final draft of the participant's enquiry will form the basis for triangulated self-/peer/tutor assessment.

A structured report for a Master's dissertation

If you are on an award-bearing course, such as a Master's course, you can use the above material to inform the writing of your dissertation. Most dissertations are about 20,000 words in length, excluding references and appendices, prelims and end matter.

Below is the conventional structure for a Master's dissertation. Although you do not have to stick to it, this structure is widely accepted in academic contexts, and you won't go far wrong if you do. Many people studying for M.Phil. and Ph.D. degrees also find this basic structure useful to inform their writing, although it is unlikely that a completed action research

Ph.D. thesis would be presented in quite this linear way. We have found that all the researchers we have supervised have created their own unique forms of presentation that accord with what Dadds and Hart (2001) have called 'methodological inventiveness':

> Perhaps the most important insight for both of us has been awareness that, for some practitioner researchers, creating their own unique way through their research may be as important as their self-chosen research focus. We had understood for many years that *substantive choice* was fundamental to the motivation and effectiveness of practitioner research (Dadds, 1995); that *what* practitioners chose to research was important to their sense of engagement and purpose. But we had understood far less well that *how* practitioners chose to research, and their sense of control over this, could be equally important to their motivation, their sense of identity within the research and their research outcomes.
>
> (Dadds and Hart, 2001: 166, emphasis in original)

Remember also that while the guidelines below act as broad outlines, you are at liberty to create your own structure, provided you address all the elements mentioned in the previous section. You may also find that aspects identified below as belonging to one chapter may go more usefully into another. There are no hard and fast rules about this. Regard the advice as outlining the jobs that need to be done. Where and how you do the jobs is up to you. Just make sure that they are done properly.

The parts of a structured report are:

- Title page
- Abstract
- Contents, including contents of appendices
- List of illustrations/figures/tables
- Acknowledgements
- Introduction
- Body of text, divided into chapters
- References
- Appendices

Guide to chapters

Abstract

Job to be done: let the reader see at a glance what the research is about, and its importance.

This consists of about 250 words. It is always written in the present tense. It outlines the structure, purposes, methods and overall significance of the work. It enables another researcher to assess whether the dissertation contains material that is relevant to their interests. It is not the place for descriptions of practice, nor for extracts from data or the literature.

Introduction

Job to be done: give an overview of why you have done this research and its potential significance.

Your introduction indicates what the report is about, its main findings and their significance. Here you explain why you wanted to do the research in terms of your educational values, and how doing the research enabled you to live in the direction of these values. You outline the main findings in terms of the evidence you have generated, and speak briefly about their significance for your own professional learning, as well as the learning of others, and the possible potentials for organisational development. In doing so, you are outlining your claim to knowledge and its significance for local and wider contexts. In general, the introduction offers an orientation guide to your reader, so that they know what they are going to encounter. It gives an overview of the report in brief terms of chapters and their contents. It may also refer to the literature that you have identified as informing your work. It is particularly helpful if you set out your research question, and then show how that question is systematically addressed throughout (but may not be answered), and how the whole study represents whatever claim to knowledge you make.

Chapter 1 Background to the research

Job to be done: focus the reader's attention on the issue you were addressing, and why.

This chapter could also be called 'Focus of the research'. You decide which chapter heading is most appropriate for you. The chapter gives reasons why you have undertaken your research, and outlines the background against which the research has been undertaken. This background is similar to the contexts (Chapter 2), but different in that it identifies the conceptual frameworks you are using in which to locate your research. 'Conceptual frameworks' is a commonly used term that refers to issues in the literature, such as social justice, democracy, gender issues, mixed-race issues, theories of change management. You may identify three or four major conceptual frameworks (possibly more), and refer to their associated literature. These issues then become part of the explanatory frameworks of your report. You need here to spell out the values that inspired you to do the research (perhaps refer back to your Introduction), and show how these values can also be located in your conceptual frameworks (possibly more), and how you are showing the development of your own understanding of these issues through doing your research. At this point you must state your research question, probably in terms of 'How do I . . .?'; for example, 'How do I ensure equal participation by all in staff meetings?' The point of this chapter is to focus the reader's attention on why you wished to do the research and how you set about doing it. You will show how your research question was informed by your values, and how the research process then became a systematic enquiry into how you could address the question, so that eventually you could make a claim that you had addressed it. It does not matter if you cannot claim that the situation may have improved because of your research. The situation may have been influenced by unforeseen circumstances. What is important is that you show your emergent understanding of your own learning, and how you have used that learning to help other people to learn.

Chapter 2　Contexts

Job to be done: provide background information on why the research needed to be done, and its potential implications.

This is where you give an outline of the contexts that inform your work. You should give information about your personal and situational contexts (who you are and where you are located), and any research and policy contexts that are relevant (what research has been undertaken in this area, and what policy recommendations exist in relation to the area). You may have other relevant personal and professional contexts which you should spell out here; for example, if you are deaf, or a member of a religious congregation, or a politician, special issues may inform your work. You may find that there is slippage between policy recommendations and real-life practice. You should not give a life history or detailed analysis, but you should include sufficient background information to help your reader understand why the research was important, and its potential relevance to future personal and organisational development.

Chapter 3 Methodology

Job to be done: provide an outline of the research design, justify your choice of design including your chosen method of enquiry, and demonstrate awareness of the need for good ethical practice.

In this chapter you give an explanation for your overall research design, which includes your choice of method of enquiry. 'Design' as used here is another way of saying 'plan'. You outline the overall plan in terms of who was involved as participants and validators, and why, where the research took place, how long it lasted, the main issues addressed, and some of the practicalities of the research that helped or hindered it. You identify and discuss the research methods used, carefully explaining the modes of data collection and analysis, the identification of criteria for judging the validity of claims and justification for their selection, how evidence was generated in relation to the criteria, and how the evidence was organised in support of your claim to knowledge. You give reasons for choosing practitioner research rather than another form of research, and also for choosing one particular approach to action research rather than another. At the same time, you show that you are consistently questioning your own assumptions. This involves demonstrating your knowledge of the different epistemological and methodological assumptions within research traditions. Because you are explaining how other people were central to your methodology, you have to outline what ethical considerations informed their involvement in your research. Describe how you distributed your ethics statement, and gained permission to do the research. You would put copies of your ethics statements and blank copies of your letters of permission into the appendices.

When you write your methodology chapter, bear in mind that what people know of your research is what you tell them. They cannot be expected to understand how you conducted your research unless you tell them. Be clear, and state the obvious.

Chapter 4 The project

Job to be done: tell the story of the research in a coherent way.

In this chapter you tell the story of your research. You present the data you have gathered and you show how you have generated evidence. It is important always to be clear about the difference between descriptions of data (what happened) and explanations of data (your interpretations, what you think was the significance of what happened). These are interdependent, but if you are clear it will help your presentation.

- **Descriptions of data** constitute an account of the progress of the research at various stages. It is useful to include here a chronological table of relevant events, graphic representations of different research cycles, and summary tables. Make sure that these tally with the action plans you outlined in your Chapter 3. If they deviated (which is often the case), explain why.
- **Interpretations of data** constitute a summary of your principal results and claims. You need to show how the claims are supported by the data, and begin to show how the data will generate, or have already generated, evidence. This means you must establish criteria by which you wish your claim to knowledge to be judged, and show how these criteria, related to your values, act consistently as the loadstars that guide your work.

Chapter 5 Significance

Job to be done: show the significance of the research and its potential implications.

Discuss the significance of your research in terms of the following:

- How has it contributed to your own personal professional learning? Are you doing things differently? Better? In what way?
- How has it contributed to the professional learning of others in your institution? Have other people been influenced by your research? Are they doing things differently? Could this collective change in practice be seen as organisational change?
- Can it make a contribution to the wider body of knowledge? In generating your own theory of practice by studying your practice, and then making your account public, can you say that you are contributing to educational theory?

Taking all these points into consideration, can you show how your research may inform future research programmes and generate useful knowledge?

References

Make sure that all your references and citations are included in your references section. Reports have been rejected in the past if they fail to observe technical conventions. Make sure you adopt the approved house style such as the Harvard system. Your tutor will give guidance about what is appropriate. Listen carefully, and follow the advice.

Appendices

This is where your raw data is presented. Appendices should be organised carefully, and labelled accurately. In the Appendices you can also indicate where your larger data archive is to be found, and what its contents are.

Note

Many exemplars of action research dissertations are now available. These include Adler-Collins (2000), Cahill (2000), Henderson (1998), Holley (1997), Larter (1987), McDermott (2001), McDonagh (2000), McGuire-Shelley (2000), Murphy (2000), Ní Mhurchú (2000), Ó Riordan-Burke (1997), O'Shea (2000), Roche (2000), Shobbrook (1997), Sullivan (2000). These and many more are available on our websites (http://www.actionresearch.net and http://www.jeanmcniff.com). Each dissertation demonstrates the authors' originality of mind and critical judgement in finding their own form of representation for their explanation of their learning in terms of their unique constellation of values. The existence of such a rich variety of accounts shows the importance of exercising originality of mind in the construction of final dissertations.

Presenting your dissertation

The following guidelines apply to most formal report writing:

- Text should be word-processed or typed using double or one and a half spacing.
- Margins 3cm on inside and 2cm at each of the remaining three.
- Pages in the main body of the text should be numbered consecutively using Arabic numerals. The introduction should be numbered separately using Roman numerals. Appendices should be numbered consecutively using Arabic numerals, and the numbers should begin at (1) at the beginning of the Appendices.
- All material must be labelled clearly. Tables and figures should have full titles. Cross-referencing must reference pages accurately.
- All quotations must be correctly referenced, including date of publication and page on which quotation appears in the original.
- Citations and references must follow the approved house style such as the Harvard system. No footnotes should be used.
- Appendices should not include raw data. Appendices should be for derived data (e.g. tables and figures not included in the main body of the text), examples of archived materials (e.g. blank copies of questionnaires), or for summaries of key meetings (e.g. validation meetings). Use

your archive for raw data and also for bulky original data such as video and audiotape-recordings. List archived material in your first Appendix.

Checklist for writing the report

The following checklist will help you to evaluate both the content and the organisation of your report.

1   Have you organised your report in such a way that the reader has easy access to the main themes and arguments? Does an explanatory statement or abstract appear at the beginning? Does the report have section headings and subheadings? Are there concluding statements/summaries?

2   Have you explained your reasons for doing the research and set out your overall aims? Is a research question evident throughout? Have you addressed it consistently? Can you show how you have generated your own theory from studying your practice?

3   Is the context of the research well described? Have you shown:
    - the importance to your workplace/institution?
    - a link with your values position?
    - links with other work and research?
    - how your research may inform future policy?

4   Have you shown how you developed a coherent action plan? Have you explained why you chose an action research methodology for conducting the research?

5   Have you described the particular techniques you used to monitor your research and gather data? Have you explained why you made those choices, and who else was involved?

6   Have you made the process of the study explicit? Have you explained how the data were generated and analysed? Have you explained the significance of the data, and shown how the data may be turned into evidence by testing them against identified criteria?

7   Have you described your validation procedures? Have you shown how formative evaluation played a part in possible action research cycles? Have you presented and discussed the outcomes of the final validation meeting? Was the authenticity, accuracy and relevance of your research agreed?

8   Have you explained the implications of the study for personal and professional practice in relation to:
    - a better understanding of your own practice?
    - how your work may contribute to organisational change?
    - how your work may contribute to the development of educational theory?

9   Have you taken all necessary care in presenting your references? Have you proofread the work at least three times?
10   Have you booked a holiday to celebrate your finished project?

Getting published

Whatever kind of report you write, it is important that it does not only occupy a space on a library shelf but is also circulated widely. Try to publish and communicate your work to others. Decide if you want to get published and then do it. Be single-minded. Don't let anything stop you. Be warned, however, that it can take a long time, often years. Even the most famous authors had to start somewhere.

Submitting papers

Target the market. Read journals. Get a feel for the style of a particular journal. Read the 'Notes to contributors' and write accordingly. Also submit your material in exactly the way that editors request. If you don't, your material may get rejected out of hand.

Be prepared to edit your work. Most papers are sent out to reviewers. Reviewers' comments are often sent to authors, and you should pay close attention to what they say. Even if you don't rework the paper entirely according to their suggestions, you should consider modifying it.

Be prepared to shorten the paper. This can be most painful, but you just have to be firm. Anything you cut at this stage can be stored for use in a later paper, so previous efforts and bright ideas are not wasted.

Writing books

Target the market. Look at the books in your field. Who publishes them? Get a feel for the style and general appearance of the books. Make a short-list of publishers you feel may be interested. Their addresses appear in their books. If not, read a reference book such as *The Writers' and Artists' Yearbook,* which contains useful addresses and information.

Once you have a good idea for your book, organise the idea as a proposal and send it to the publisher, usually the editor for your special field. Aim to produce three or four sides of A4 paper using the following headings.

- Rationale for the book
- About the author (you)
- Contents of the book
- Possible market (and possible marketing outlets such as your own networks and professional organisations)

- Why your book is needed
- Competition – what other books similar to yours are available, and why yours is significant
- Time-line for writing the book

Include some sample writing. This could be one or two chapters, or extracts from several chapters. The editor needs to see what your writing is like. Most publishing houses provide guidelines for potential authors, so contact them or access their websites, and follow their requirements.

If you think this is a tall order, remember that editors are bombarded with proposals. It is a highly competitive business, and budgets are limited. Therefore you have to sell your work to the publisher, as they will in turn have to sell it to customers. Your book is something special, so tell people how special it is and why they must read it.

People who publish their work tend to be compulsive writers. They have to be, because books are seldom written in one go, and involve substantial amounts of editing and redrafting. This can take months, even years. Allow plenty of time. Get on with it, though. Someone else may get the ideas out before you!

Also allow plenty of time for the book to appear. When it leaves you, you will see it only once again, at proofreading stage. After that you can expect to wait months before it appears as a book.

But when it does, there is nothing quite so thrilling as to hear the thump of a book on the mat or to see your name in print. All that hard work, from when you began your project to now that it is there in the public domain, has been worthwhile. All the effort and time were for something. You have produced a work of value and have made a productive contribution to the world, and you can feel affirmed when others acknowledge that they have found value in your ideas and your influence is felt in their lives.

Well done! Now for the next project.

References

Adler-Collins, J. (2000) 'A scholarship of enquiry.' MA dissertation, University of Bath. Available at http://www.bath.ac.uk/~edsajw/jekan/shtml.

Atkinson, E. (2000) 'Behind the inquiring mind: Exploring the transition from external to internal inquiry', *Reflective Practice* 1(2): 149–64.

Bai, H. (2001) 'Beyond the educated mind: towards a pedagogy of mindfulness', in B. Hocking, J. Haskell and W. Linds (eds) *Unfolding Bodymind: Exploring Possibility Through Education*. Brandon, Foundation for Educational Renewal.

Bayne-Jardine, C. and Holly, P. (1994) *Developing Quality Schools*. London, Falmer.

Belenky, M., Clinchy, B., Goldberger, B. and Tarule, J. (1986) *Women's Ways of Knowing*. New York, Basic Books.

Berlin, I. (1998) *The Proper Study of Mankind: An Anthology of Essays*. London, Pimlico.

Bosher, M. (2001) 'How can I, as an educator and professional development manager working with teachers, support and enhance the learning and achievement of pupils in a Whole School Improvement Process?' Ph.D. thesis, University of Bath. Available at http://www.bath.ac.uk/~edsajw/bosher.shtml.

Boud, D. and Griffin, V. (1987) *Appreciating Adults Learning*. London, Kogan Page.

Bourdieu, P. (1990) *The Logic of Practice*. London, Polity Press.

Brennan, E. (1994) 'Teaching German to a poorly motivated first year class', in J. McNiff and Ú. Collins (eds) *A New Approach to In-Career Development for Teachers in Ireland*. Bournemouth, Hyde. Available at http://www.jeanmcniff.com.

Bullough, R.V. and Pinnegar, S. (2001) 'Guidelines for quality in autobiographical forms of self-study', *Educational Researcher* 30(2): 13–21.

Cahill, M. (2000) 'How can I encourage pupils to participate in their own learning?' MA dissertation, Thurles, University of the West of England, Bristol. Available on http://www.jeanmcniff.com.

Clandinin, J. and Connelly, M. (2000) *Narrative Inquiry: Experience and Story in Qualitative Research*. San Francisco, CA, Jossey-Bass.

Cluskey, M. (1996) 'The paradigms of educational research and how they relate to my practice', *Action Researcher* 4: 1–4.

Collingwood, R. (1939) *An Autobiography*. Oxford, Oxford University Press.

Connelly, M. and Clandinin, J. (1990) 'Stories of experience and narrative enquiry', *Educational Researcher* 19(5): 2–14.

Dadds, M. (1995) *Passionate Enquiry and School Development: A Story About Teacher Action Research*. London, Falmer.

Dadds, M. and Hart, S. (2001) *Doing Practitioner Research Differently*. London, RoutledgeFalmer.

Delong, J. (2002) 'How can I improve my practice as a superintendent of schools and create my own living educational theory?' Ph.D. thesis, University of Bath. Available on http://www.bath.ac.uk/~edsajw/delong.shtml.

Dewey, J. (1938) *Experience and Education*. New York, Macmillan.

Diamond, P. (1988) 'Biography as a tool for self-understanding.' Paper presented at a staff seminar, University of Surrey.

Elliott, J. (1991) *Action Research for Educational Change*. Milton Keynes, Open University Press.

Evans, M. (1993a) 'An action research enquiry into my role as a deputy head-teacher in a comprehensive school.' Transfer report from M.Phil. to Ph.D., Kingston, Kingston University.

Evans, M. (1993b) 'Using story as an aid to reflection in an action research cycle: just tell me what to do.' Paper presented at the British Educational Research Association Annual Conference, Liverpool.

Fletcher, S. (2000) *Mentoring in Schools*. London, Kogan Page.

Follows, M. (1989) 'The development of co-operative teaching in a semi-open-plan infant school', in P. Lomax (ed.) *The Management of Change*. Clevedon, Multi-Lingual Matters.

Fromm, E. (1979) *To Have or to Be*. New York, Abacus.

Gardner, H. (1983) *Frames of Mind: The Theory of Multiple Intelligences*. New York, Basic Books.

Geraci, J. (2001) 'Towards an understanding of autism: an outsider's attempt to get inside', in M. Dadds and S. Hart *Doing Practitioner Research Differently*. London, RoutledgeFalmer.

Griffiths, M. (1990) 'Action research: grass roots practice or management tool?', in P. Lomax (ed.) *Managing Staff Development in Schools: An Action Research Approach*. Clevedon, Multi-Lingual Matters.

Hannon, D. (1996) 'Preparing student teachers to respond to special educational needs: science boxes for children being taught at home or in hospital', in P. Lomax (ed.) *Quality Management in Education*. London, Routledge.

Henderson, C. (1998) 'How can I become a more effective adult educator and teach information technology appropriately?' MA dissertation, Dublin, University of the West of England, Bristol. Available at http://www.jeanmcniff.com.

Hewitt, T. (1994) 'Networking in action research communities', *Action Researcher* 1: 35.

Holley, E. (1997) 'How do I as a teacher-researcher contribute to the development of a living educational theory through an exploration of my values in my professional practice?' M.Phil. thesis, University of Bath. Available at http://www.bath.ac.uk/~edsajw/erica.shtml.

Ingram, P. (2001) 'Pauline and Alzheimer's: "reflections" on caring', in R. Winter and C. Munn-Giddings *A Handbook for Action Research in Health and Social Care*. London, Routledge.

Jones, B. (1989) 'In conversation with myself: becoming an action researcher', in P. Lomax (ed.) *The Management of Change*. Clevedon, Multi-Lingual Matters.

Kemmis, S. and McTaggart, R. (1982) *The Action Research Planner*. Goolong, Deakin University Press.

Kilpatrick, W. (1951) 'Critical issues in current educational theory', *Educational Theory* 1(1): 18.

Larter, A. (1987) 'An action research approach to classroom discussion in the examination years.' M.Phil. thesis, University of Bath. Available at http://www.bath.ac.uk/~edsajw/andy.html.

Lewin, K. (1946) 'Action research and minority problems', *Journal of Social Issues* 2: n.p.

Linter, R. (1989) 'Improving classroom interaction: an action research study', in P. Lomax (ed.) *The Management of Change*. Clevedon, Multi-Lingual Matters.

Lomax, P. (1994a) 'Action research for managing change', in N. Bennett, R. Glatter and R. Levacic (eds) *Improving Educational Management through Research and Consultancy*. London, Paul Chapman/Open University Press.

Lomax, P. (1994b) 'Standards, criteria and the problematic of action research', *Educational Action Research* 2(1): 113–25.

Lomax, P. and Parker, Z. (1995) 'Accounting for ourselves: the problematics of representing action research', in *Cambridge Journal of Education* 25(3): 301–14.

Lomax, P., Woodward, C. and Parker, Z. (1996) 'Critical friends, collaborative working and strategies for effecting quality', in P. Lomax (ed.) *Quality Management in Education*. London, Routledge and Hyde.

McCormack, C. (2002) 'Action research in the home', in J. McNiff *Action Research: Principles and Practice* (2nd edn). London, RoutledgeFalmer.

McDaniel, M. (2002) 'The professional as researcher.' Assignment for Module on Ed.D. Programme, Queen's University Belfast. Available at http://www.jeanmcniff.com

McDermott, K. (2002) 'Reading practice: essays in dialogue and pedagogical conversations.' Ph.D. thesis, University of Glamorgan.

McDermott, P. (2001) 'How can I improve my practice as an adult literacy organiser?' MA dissertation, Dublin, University of the West of England, Bristol. Available at http://www.jeanmcniff.com.

Mc Donagh, C. (2000) 'Towards a theory of professional teacher voice: How can I improve my teaching of pupils with specific learning difficulties in the area of language?' MA dissertation, Dublin, University of the West of England, Bristol. Available at http://www.jeanmcniff.com.

McGuire-Shelley, M. (2000) 'How can I assist children discover the "Me" in environment?' MA dissertation, Thurles, University of the West of England, Bristol. Available on http://www.jeanmcniff.com.

McNiff, J. (1990) 'Writing and the creation of educational knowledge', in P. Lomax (ed.) *Managing Staff Development in Schools: An Action Research Approach*. Clevedon, Multi-Lingual Matters.

McNiff, J. with J. Whitehead (2000) *Action Research in Organisations*. London, Routledge.

McNiff, J. with J. Whitehead (2002) *Action Research: Principles and Practice* (2nd edn). London, RoutledgeFalmer.

McTaggart, R. (1990) 'Involving a whole staff in developing a maths curriculum', in P. Lomax (ed.) *Managing Staff Development in Schools: An Action Research Approach.* Clevedon, Multi-Lingual Matters.

McTiernan, M. (1997) 'How do I improve my practice as a teacher of adults?' MA dissertation, Dublin, University of the West of England, Bristol. Available at http://www.jeanmcniff.com.

Mead, G. (2001) 'Unlatching the gate: realising my scholarship of living inquiry.' Ph.D. thesis, University of Bath. Available at http://www.bath.ac.uk/~edsajw/mead.shtml.

Mellor, N. (1998) 'Notes from a method', *Educational Action Research* 6(3): 453–70.

Mills, G. (2000) *Action Research: A Guide for the Teacher Researcher.* Princeton, NJ, Prentice Hall.

Murphy, P. (2000) 'How I developed a practice and learnt to conduct it more effectively.' MA dissertation, Dublin, University of the West of England, Bristol.

Ní Mhurchú (2000) 'How can I improve my practice as a teacher in the area of assessment through the use of portfolios?' MA dissertation, Cork, University of the West of England, Bristol. Reprinted in abridged form in J. McNiff (2002) *Action Research: Principles and Practice.* London, RoutledgeFalmer. Complete version available at http://www.jeanmcniff.com.

Nonaka, I. and Takeuchi, H. (1995) *The Knowledge-Creating Company: How Japanese Companies Create the Dynamics of Innovation.* Oxford, Oxford University Press.

Ó Muimhneacháin, C. (2002) 'Expect the unexpected', in J. McNiff *Action Research: Principles and Practice* (2nd edn). London, RoutledgeFalmer.

Ó Riordan-Burke, T. (1997) 'How can I improve my practice as a learning support teacher?' MA dissertation, Dublin, University of the West of England, Bristol. Available at http://www.jeanmcniff.com. and http://www.actionresearch.net.

O'Shea, K. (2000) 'Coming to know my own practice.' MA dissertation, Dublin, University of the West of England, Bristol. Available on http://www.jeanmcniff.com.

Overboe, J. (2001) 'Creating a space for embodied wisdom through teaching', in B. Hocking, J. Haskell and W. Linds (eds) *Unfolding Bodymind: Exploring Possibility Through Education.* Brandon, Foundation for Educational Renewal.

Parker, Z. (1993) 'Where do I go next on my journey to improve my practice as a researcher?' Paper presented at the British Educational Research Association Annual Conference, Liverpool.

Parker, Z. (1994) 'Making sense of interview data within the aims of an action research study.' Paper presented at the Collaborative Action Research Network Conference, Birmingham.

Perselli, V. (2002a) 'What might the performance modality have to say to/in higher education?' Performance and paper presented at the British Educational Research Association Annual Conference, Exeter.

Perselli, V. (2002b) 'Performance: "A personal preview": reconceptualising our practices as teachers through visual imagery and imaginative conjecture.' Performance and paper presented at the American Educational Research Association Annual Meeting, New Orleans.

Polanyi, M. (1958) *Personal Knowledge.* London, Routledge & Kegan Paul.

Popper, K. (1963) *Conjectures and Refutations: The Growth of Scientific Knowledge.* London, Routledge & Kegan Paul.

Popper, K. (1972) *Objective Knowledge: An Evolutionary Approach.* Oxford, Oxford University Press.

Pring, R. (2000) *Philosophy of Educational Research.* London, Continuum.

Prosser, J. (ed.) (1998) *Image-based Research: A Sourcebook for Qualitative Researchers.* London, Falmer.

Robson, C. (1993) *Real World Research: A Resource for Social Scientists and Practitioner-Researchers.* Oxford, Blackwell.

Roche, M. (2000) 'How can I improve my practice so as to help my pupils to philosophise?' Unpublished MA dissertation, Cork, University of the West of England, Bristol. Available at http://www.jeanmcniff.com.

Russell, T. and Korthagen, F. (1995) *Teachers Who Teach Teachers.* London, Falmer.

Schön, D. (1983) *The Reflective Practitioner: How Professionals Think in Action.* New York, Basic Books.

Schön, D. (1995) 'Knowing-in-action: The new scholarship requires a new epistemology', *Change,* November to December: 2734.

Schratz, M. (2000) 'Towards a new architecture of learning: reflections on action as an experience of change', in J. McNiff, G. McNamara and D. Leonard (eds) *Action Research in Ireland.* Dorset, September.

Shobbrook, H. (1997) 'My living educational theory grounded in my life: How can I enable my communication through correspondence to be seen as educational and worthy of presentation in its original form?' MA dissertation, University of Bath. Available at http://www.bath.ac.uk/~edsajw/hilary.shtml.

Stenhouse, L. (1978) 'Case study and case records: towards a contemporary history of education', *British Educational Research Journal* 4(2): 21–39.

Sternberg, R. and Horvath, J. (1999) *Tacit Knowledge in Professional Practice: Researcher and Practitioner Perspectives.* Mahwah, NJ, Lawrence Erlbaum Associates.

Sullivan, B. (2000) 'How can I help my pupils to make more effective use of their time in school?' MA dissertation, Dublin, University of the West of England, Bristol. Available at http://www.jeanmcniff.com.

Sullivan, B. (2002) 'How do I improve my practice as a teacher of Traveller children?' Working paper, Limerick, University of Limerick.

Whitehead, J. (1985) 'An analysis of an individual's educational development: the basis for personally oriented action research', in M. Shipman *Educational Research: Principles, Policies and Practice.* Basingstoke, Falmer Press.

Whitehead, J. (1989) 'Creating a living educational theory from questions of the kind, "How do I improve my practice?"', *Cambridge Journal of Education* 19(1): 41–52.

Whitehead, J. (1993) *The Growth of Educational Knowledge: Creating Your Own Living Educational Theories.* Bournemouth, Hyde.

Whitehead, J. and Delong, J. (2003) 'Knowledge-creation in educational leadership and administration through teacher-research', in A. Clarke and G. Erikson (eds) *Teacher Inquiry: Living the research in everyday practice.* London, Routledge-Falmer.

Winter, R. and Munn-Giddings, C. (2001) *A Handbook for Action Research in Health and Social Care.* London, Routledge.

Winter, R., Sobiechowska, P. and Buck, A. (1999) *Professional Experience and the Investigative Imagination.* London, Routledge.

Zeni, J. (2001) *Ethical Issues in Practitioner Research.* New York, Teachers College Press.

Index